Sanitation in India : A Historico-Sociological Survey

Sanitation in India : A Historico-Sociological Survey

Hetukar Jha
Former Professor of Sociology
Patna University

GYAN

ISBN: 978-81-2121-278-6

Price: 290/-

Published by

Gyan Books (P) Ltd.
Gyan Kunj, 5, Ansari Road,
Daryaganj, Delhi – 110052
E-mail: books@gyanbooks.com
Mob.: 9811692060

Laser Typesetting: Lucky Graphic, Delhi

Printed at: G. Print Process, Delhi

Cataloging in Publication Data-DK

Courtesy : D.K. Agencies (P) Ltd.<docinfo@ dkagencies.com>

Jha, Hetukar, 1944- author.

Sanitation in India : a historico-sociological survey/by

Hetukar Jha.

Pages cm

Includes bibliographical references.

ISBN 9788121212786

1. Sanitation-India-History. 2. Sanitation-Social aspects-India. 3.

Dalits-India. 1. Title.

DDC 363.720954 23

Dedicated to

Padma Bhushan Dr. Bindeshwar Pathak,
A Conspicuous Gandhian Crusader

Foreword

This insightful book, 'Sanitation in India: A Historico-Sociological Survey' by Prof. Hetukar Jha, former Professor of Sociology, Patna University, is the upshot of a two-day national workshop organised by Sulabh International Social Service Organisation on January 28 and 29, 2013 in New Delhi on 'Sociology of Sanitation' in which social scientists, reformers and a galaxy of luminaries from all over the country had august participation and unrolled their views. I do feel that 'Sociology of Sanitation' in India should be nurtured and devoted as desideratum in Indian sociology to make the people conscious of the abiding import of sanitation as well as how it was observed aeons ago. The odyssey of sanitation right from the Ancient India will be very salutary for the amelioration of the quality of life and dignity of the social ethos.

'Sanitation in India: A Historico-Sociological Survey' comprising three chapters namely 'Introduction', 'Sanitation and Society in the Colonial Period' and 'Untouchability and Sanitation in Pre-Modern Era' followed by Appendix A and Appendix B sheds ample light on the changing trends in the study of sociology which now rivets our gaze more on the publicly relevant issues that encompass the people who have been overlooked, discouraged, marginalised, insulted and injured. Now the time is to recognise the importance of those who clean the dirt rather than of those who create or spread the dirt. From time immemorial the people engaged in cleaning work have been deemed pariahs but it is high time in the 21st century democratic India we recognised the paramount importance of purification in all endeavours of our life. Unclean drinking water, inadequate sewage disposal, various types of diseases raging through mosquitoes that stem from the filth and dirt, leprosy, cholera etc. can be conquered if proper attention is paid to sanitation and hygiene - the sine-qua-non of human society.

The author of this unputdownable book has furnished scientific data and has also cited copious reports of Sulabh International, WHO, UNICEF etc. regarding the gravest sanitation problem i.e. disposal of human excreta, inadequate maintenance of water and sewerage systems which engender serious health hazards. In order to tide over these vexing problems people should be made aware and given basic education about the importance of sanitation. The NGOs and the government organizations should forge ahead to tackle the problems of sanitation and hygiene effectively. Different types of programmes like School Sanitation and Hygiene Education Programme (SSHE), Education Project, Sarva Siksha Abhiyan etc. ought to be kept running throughout with austere honesty, integrity and accountability.

'Sanitation and Society in the Colonial Period' has been devoted to the study of idioms and proverbs in different parts of the country, particularly Bihar, regarding the premium granted to sanitation from the ancient period. The studies made by different savants and scholars from time to time, for example, G.A. Grierson, William Hodges, and Francis Buchanan and a lot of reports published in various journals and magazines tell us about the circumstances under which the poor people of the lower castes and tribes joined the profession of manual scavenging in different periods for their survival. As they were engrossed in cleaning work, they should have been allowed due respect but the irony of the society is that they were declared untouchables, lepers and slaves and were coerced to take human excreta on their heads. Their condition worsened and remained the same for centuries. Seeing their abject plight Gandhiji spearheaded the mission of abolishing untouchability since 1915 by improving their cultural, social and educational conditions. Different organizations came into existence in this field and gradually Bhangi Mukti and abolition of the tradition of untouchability were given legal strength.

'Untouchablity and Sanitaiton in Pre-Modern Era' brings to the horrendous condition of the sewerage system and the plight of the scavengers in India. In ancient India at some of the places where excavations have been done, archaeological findings betray that the drainage system was well developed. Hastinapur, Kaushambi, Mathura, Rajghat, Pataliputra, Chirand (near Chapra in Bihar) etc. were glaring examples of good town planning. Maybe, later on due to the spiralling population the drainage system and well-planned town system might have been brushed aside and for the cleaning work, people hinged on human labour and the people doing cleaning work were eyed as out-castes or untouchables. Dr. Hetukar Jha has quoted lines from the works of eminent scholars such as A.S. Altekar, Debi Prasad Chattopadhyaya, Hazari Prasad Dwivedi, R.S. Sharma, R.K. Choudhary and a host of others to prove how caste system and untouchability got strengthened. It is due to the strong caste system and some of interpolated lines espousing this system in the religious books that the untouchablity ensued and occasioned a sense of social hate and contempt for the Brahmanical order in which 'Janmana Jati' overpowered 'Karmana Jati'. I would point out that no work is mean and no person involved in any calling is high or low. Every profession should be respected and there should be no discrimination in our society on the score of caste or creed.

The profession of cleaning and scavenging should be given as much respect as we give to the profession of doctors, teachers, lawyers or public servants. Every profession is to impart immense strength to our society and it is only by respecting the people of all professions that we can make India a great and ideal nation. In order to put premium on the importance of sanitation, the slogan 'Toilets first, temples later' put forward by our Prime Minister Mr. Narendra Modi is very pertinent. There is a grounding swell for 'Swacch Bharat' which will cement the nation.

The author of this book has added some of the pages (pp 136-149) of Grihastha Ratnakar in original as Appendix A and the Hindi translation of the same as Appendix B. They are very pertinent. 'Mutrapurishotsarga' of Grihastha Ratnakar makes us aware of the lines quoted from Vishnu Purana, Sankhayayana, Grihasutra, Brahmanda Purana, Smriti Samuchaya, Brahma Purana etc. regarding sanitation, cleanliness and how, when and in which direction should we do ablution and then clean our different parts of the body. The lines uttered by Manu, Baudhyana, Yama, Harit, Vasishtha, Daksha Muni, Shankh Muni, Paithinasi and a host of others are important and timely as they put stress on the importance of sanitation, cleanliness and making the ambience clean.

This book written in simple, lucid, and vivid prose, I am sure, will benefit the people a lot and will make them conscious of sanitation and purification. As 'proper words are in proper places', the book is an interesting read.

-Dr. Bindeshwar Pathak
Ph.D., D.Litt.

Preface

The present work covers a long period from ancient to contemporary eras. The attempt has been made to describe broadly the conditions of sanitation in different periods. However, in this context, generally, the regions of north India have received more attention. Besides, paucity of material made it difficult to analyse precisely the socio-economic forces which gave rise to and nurtured the association of untouchability with sanitation.

The present treatise may be supposed to be just preliminary, though attempt has been made to discuss in detail as far as possible the traditions linking untouchability with sanitation in different periods of our history. However, it seems necessary to point out that the project of research on this issue (the roots and prevalence of association of untouchability and sanitation) has to be relatively long, exploratory and multidisciplinary. Sanitation in varying contexts of time and space of our civilization is yet to be recognized as a very important field of academic research and study. Since the last few years of the last century, quite a number of intellectuals began to urge the necessity for devoting attention to the overlooked and ignored. So, Dr. Bindeshwar Pathak's call for developing 'Sociology of Sanitation' seems to accord well with this trend. I owe a deep debt of gratitude to him for granting me an opportunity of undertaking this survey.

Quite a number of friends helped me as and when I required their assistance. I am thankful to all of them. Pt. Shashi Nath Jha, professor of Vyakarana, K.S.D. Sanskrit University, Darbhanga, translated into Hindi the details of ancient and medieval Dharmashastra norms and regulations (relating to defecation and ablution after voiding excrement) narrated in Sanskrit in the famous digest, Grihastha Ratnakara of early fourteenth century. I am indebted to him. Paras Nath Singh Thakur typed the manuscript on computer quite efficiently. My thanks are due to him.

Hetukar Jha

Contents

Introduction

In January, 2013, Dr. Bindeshwar Pathak, founder of Sulabh International Social Service Organisation and the renowned leader of Sulabh movement for improving public health, environmental sanitation and, what is, perhaps, more important, for obliterating the tradition that affords the most dishonoured space for a particular community granting it the epithet bhangi, voiced a nation-wide appeal for thinking of and developing 'sociology of sanitation' as one of the fields of Indian sociology that would help in the generation of knowledge of the traditions relating to the different aspects of sanitation in different periods and parts of the country. Such knowledge, he further contended, shall also be useful for planning and executing the strategies required for engineering quite efficiently the changes desirable for improving the quality of life and dignity of all in our society[1]. In the National Workshop organized on January 28 and 29, 2013, all the social scientists and social workers, who participated in this workshop, endorsed unequivocally the proposal of Dr. Pathak. He, then, suggested the attendees to come forward and prepare books/articles for teaching and research in the field of sociology of sanitation. The present endeavour has been undertaken in response to his appeal.

Why should there be 'sociology of sanitation' in India ? This question has to be dealt with first by discussing the present state of sociological thinking. In this context, it may be said that until about the 1960s sociology was regarded[2] "as an endeavour largely empty of intellectual content... characteristically dominated by a rather complacent conception that human institutions can be analysed by methods parallel to those employed in the natural sciences;... and (was) typically associated with a cosy, ethnocentric vision of an increasingly abundant future to be brought about through the progressive spread of industrialism". However, by the end of the 1950s, C. Wright Mills introduced the idea of 'sociological imagination' pleading in favour of a perspective opposed to the one dominated by[3] "methodological pretensions... which trivialize.. (sociology/social sciences) by concern with minor problems unconnected with publicly relevant issues" (emphasis added). His approach, it seems, began to be appreciated by a wide circle of sociologists[4]. Reflecting on Mills's perspective by the end of the 1980s, Anthony Giddens wrote[5] that "the sociological imagination necessitates, above all, being able to 'think ourselves away' from the familiar routines of our daily lives in order to look at them anew... Developing the sociological imagination means using materials from anthropology... and history... The past is a mirror which the sociologist must hold up to understand the present... (that) involves 'thinking ourselves away' from our customs and habits – in order to develop a more profound understanding... The imaginative pursuit of sociological work can show us not just what is the case, but what could become the case..." Mills thus urged that sociology should be historical drawing materials from anthropology and history in order to develop a profound understanding of "publicly relevant issues" that could also help in shaping the future of society.

Besides, since the 1970s as a result of the growing disillusionment with the developmental models of modernization[6], increasing appeal of the theoretical standpoints favouring common conceptual concerns of sociology and history[7], and emerging view of the underdevelopment of the large part of globe as a consequence of colonialism and imperialism, etc., sociological studies of past socio-economic, political and cultural conditions began to be undertaken giving rise to macro-historical sociology[8]. Underdevelopment characterizing the vast area of world was, "publicly relevant issue" (in the words of Mills, mentioned before) that prompted such intellectuals as I. Wallerstein, Janet Abu-Lughod, Charles Tilly, Michael Mann and many others to study the past from the points of view of the present for understanding and reflecting on the crisis of the vast mass of people living today[9]. Gradually, it seems, the notion of "publicly relevant issue" came to include the conditions of existence of the ordinary and taken for granted, the overlooked, the discouraged, the prohibited and the deprived / disadvantaged, for sociological investigation from historical perspective[10]. It may be pointed out in this context that more or less a similar trend is visible to some extent in Indian sociology as well[11]. One may, thus, contend that the awful and precarious conditions of sanitation and the community associated with it for the last many centuries also constitute 'publicly relevant issue' by all means and, therefore, deserve to be subjected to historio-sociological studies for developing a profound and appropriate understanding of how and to which extent they prevailed before and survive today. Such an understanding can, hopefully, also contribute to the planning of an efficient strategy of tackling them effectively.

Sanitation is recognized as one of the most 'publicly relevant issues' in India now. According to Oxford Dictionary of English, it refers to the "conditions relating to public health, especially the provision of clean drinking water and adequate sewage disposal". In the context of both (provision of clean drinking water and that of adequate sewage disposal), the situation appears to be alarming in our country. The problem is more acute and complex due to the traditional practice associating a particular community with the system of sewage disposal. Soon after Independence, Gunnar Myrdal took note of massive incidence of leprosy, cholera, etc., and observed that[12] "...efforts to prevent and cure disease will increasingly found sanitary conditions quite inferior being of very low level[13]: "only about 6% of India's total population had access to protected water supply... the percentage of its rural population thus supplied must be negligible... Disposing of human excreta is perhaps the gravest sanitation problem. Proper latrines are extremely rare... Inadequate maintenance of newly constructed water and sewer systems has frequently created further health hazards". For improving the public hygiene, he recommended that masses must be educated[14]: "People must be taught to be more rational and more concerned about their health". In this context, he referred to Gandhi, who[15] "upbraided his people for their unhygienic habits and for the filth found in temples, streets and private homes... (He) demonstrated his faith... by himself breaking the taboos against scavenging. He believed that "basic education' should include the elementary principles of sanitation, hygiene.." (emphasis added). The state of sanitation, however, still continues to be depressing.

According to one report[16], "The severity of the problem in India could be judged from the fact that hardly 33% population have sanitation facility available. In rural area percentage coverage is only 22". India, it is reported[17], "is faced with the formidable task of handling 900 million litres of urine and 135 million kg of faecal matter per day with a totally inadequate system of collection and disposal. In most of the urban areas even on the streets where sewers have been laid, houses have not been connected... insanitation continues. In the rural areas, 102 million households have no toilet facilities at all". According to a recent report[18], the total number of public toilets is only 1800 in Delhi; the number of public urinals in Mumbai is also not quite adequate, only around 1100; but the situation is more alarming in state capital cities, for example, there are only 100 public urinals in Patna for the population of 16.83 lakh. One can gauge the condition of small cities/towns and rural areas.

Further, it is reported that two-thirds of the Indian population go out for defecation in the open areas and over 120 million houses do not have toilet facilities[19]. So far as the state/district – wise details regarding the lack of toilet facilities, drinking water, sewage disposal system, etc., are concerned, much light has been thrown on these problems by national and international organizations such as Sulabh International, WHO,UNICEF, etc., which implicitly or explicitly confirm the urgent need of recognizing sanitation as a 'publicly relevant issue' by people, government, and academics as well. The attention of social scientists, it seems, is being increasingly drawn towards this issue. For example, Deen Spears, an economist, has recently worked on the consequences of the practice of defecation in the open. According to him[20], "More than half of all people in the world who defecate in the open live in India... 53% of households do not use any kind of toilet or latrine... No country measured in the last ten years has a higher rate of open defecation than Bihar. Twelve percent of all people worldwide who openly defecate live in Uttar Pradesh....... Poor sanitation is not the only threat to Indian children's health... <u>But evidence suggests that socially privileged and disadvantaged children alike are shorter than they would be in the absence of open defecation</u>" (emphasis added).

A senior and experienced physician of Bihar observes in the context and the widely prevalent practice of open defecation that[21] "The perception goes that villages don't need toilet since they have large areas of open spaces. Now that village roads have come up, villagers are using them as open toilets. Consequently, there is filth and (there are) diseases. Besides the environmental pollution and the contamination of food and water it causes, <u>just think of the plight of women. They cannot ease themselves when they get the urge and often</u>

have to wait until the evening, after it gets dark. They end up suffering from bladder and bowel problems" (emphasis added). The miserable experience of women living in villages due to the absence of toilets has also been narrated by Shefalika Verma in her autobiography (in Maithili)[22]. It may be mentioned in this context that according to a report of P. Banerji (published in Hindustan, Patna, June 19, 2014, p13), 69.3% of rural households in India have no toilet and, consequently, the National Human Rights Commission asserts that women going out for defecation in the open generally fall victim to rape.

Awareness of the grave threat to environment and public health due to the depressing conditions of sanitation, it seems, is widely shared by different categories of people who have now begun to raise their voice for tackling this crisis. For example[23], "Members of Parliament, civil society organizations and campaigners from India, Pakistan, Bangladesh, Nepal, Bhutan and Sri Lanka marched towards the SAARC secretariat in Kathmandu on Tuesday demanding 'Right to Sanitation for All'. Calling upon the SAARC countries to 'Speak in One Voice' at the 18th SAARC summit to be held in Nepal this year, the entourage submitted a 'Citizens Charter' stressing on recognizing sanitation as a legal right. The Charter urges the governments of South Asia to spend at least one percent of the GDP to achieve universal sanitation... Around 69% of the people in Nepal, 66% in India, 63% in Afghanistan... are denied access to improved sanitation... 'Around one billion people in South Asia... do not use toilets and 700 million people defecate in the open', said Mustafa Talpur, regional manager, Water-Aid... A year-long 'Keep Your Promises' campaign was also launched to accelerate progress on sanitation and hygiene... 'Eliminate all forms of manual scavenging and ensure dignity and equality for the sanitation workforce', the Charter adds...".

for mobilizing government(s) for improving the conditions of sanitation (described above), some of the NGOs have been working seriously in this context. For example, Sulabh International Social Service Organization[24], "a pioneering NGO in Sanitation in India, developed cost-effective sanitation technologies for household and community use with onsite safe disposal system, which not only promotes safe sanitation but also prevents environmental degradation. The NGO also developed technologies for water-effluent treatment..." Under the leadership of Dr. Bindeshwar Pathak, Sulabh's achievements may be considered quite significant. More than 600 towns are free from scavenging problem; about a million scavengers have been virtually liberated from their age-old task of carrying nightsoil; sanitation facilities developed by Sulabh are used every day by lakhs of people in different corners of India[25].

Who can deny the value and genuineness of the concern of civil society organizations, political representatives, and other public bodies for sanitation? The malaise, however, is deeper than what is visible. According to a report of K. Hemlatha (The Times of India, Patna, June 19, 2014, p. 17), "Social workers say there is a big cultural barrier that stops people especially in rural areas from using toilets – and that no amount of government schemes and programmes will succeed unless people are convinced toilets are hygienic". About four decades back, Gunnar Myrdal had expressed more or less the same view that[26] "The improvement of public hygiene is.. not merely a problem of acquiring.. financial resources. It is a problem of educating the masses" (emphasis added). Gandhi took a bold step by breaking the taboos against scavenging. He, however, believed that[27] "'basic education' should include the elementary principles of sanitation, hygiene..." His close associate, Pyre Lal asserted in this context in 1950[28] "...that if we mean business we should introduce the Science and Art of

Scavenging and Sanitation as... essential item in the curricula of our educational institutions. There is no reason why there should not be a faculty of municipal and village sanitation and scavenging in our universities too.. (emphasis edded)" Considering the value of education as a means for tackling the problems of sanitation and hygiene, 'School Sanitation and Hygiene Education Program' (SSHE) was started in Bihar as a component of Bihar Education Project/Sarva Siksha Abhiyan. No doubt, creation of facilities and classroom instruction are important for changing the insanitary and unhygienic conditions. But more important in this context is to realize that the age-long habit or practice of open defecation is a cultural problem and, therefore, it is necessary to generate knowledge of how and when, in which socio-economic circumstances, habits and practices related to defecation, disposal of sewage, disposal of dirt and dead bodies, association of particular caste groups with scavenging, etc., developed and gained ground affecting public health, environment and the moral face of society at large quite adversely. Such knowledge can, hopefully, yield appropriate insight into these problems for tackling them successfully on a long term (or permanent) basis. And, for developing such knowledge, following the approach of C. Wright Mills (discussed before), different traditions (in different parts of the country) relating to the conditions of sanitation, hygiene, scavenging, etc., should be rather increasingly subjected to historico-sociological studies. In this context, the words of D.P. Mukeji are quite inspiring. In his Presidential Address to All India Sociological Conference in 1955, he pointed out that our socio-cultural reality is unique or different from that of Western societies; for us, our traditions are the living embodiment of the social nature of Indian culture and the first task of Indian sociologists is to study our traditions because even for changing traditions

Indian sociology suggested, the contention of C. Wright Mills for developing sociological imagination and the current trend of sociology favouring the study of the ignored, the call for developing 'sociology of sanitation' as a sub-discipline of Indian sociology seems to be justified by all means. For pursuing the venture of historico-sociological study of sanitation in India, it will not be out of place to discuss at least briefly the conditions of sanitation which prevailed in past centuries. In the second chapter, an attempt has been made for covering the colonial period (since the second half of the eighteenth century) in this context. In the third chapter, a synoptic survey of pre-modern era (from ancient to medieval periods) is presented for understanding the practices related to sanitation and hygiene. However, it may be urged here that studies in the field of sociology of sanitation should be increasingly undertaken more rigorously both at micro and macro levels for generating profound knowledge not only of the different aspects of the present conditions (of sanitation), but, also of how and when did they emerge and gain ground in our society.

Notes :

1. See his letter no. SICAS/SOS/191/2013 of January 8, 2013.
2. Giddens, Anthony 1981:15 "The State of Sociology", The Times Literary Supplement (henceforth TLS), No. 4065, February, pp. 215-216.
3. Mills, C. Wright 1969:20 The Sociological Imagination New York, London, Oxford : The Oxford University Press (Paperback edn.) ; first published 1959.
4. It is indicated by the publication of his book (The Sociological Imagination) again in 1970 (Harmondsworth : Penguin).
5. Giddens, Anthony 1990:20-21 Sociology, Cambridge : Polity Press, first published 1989.
6. See Tilly, Charles 1980 "Historical Sociology" Current Perspectives in Social Theory, Vol. I, pp. 55-59.
7. See Giddens, Anthony 1981 "The State of Sociology", TLS No. 4065, February 27, pp. 215-216.
8. See Tilly, Charles 2007 "Three Versions of History and Theory", History and Theory, 46 May, pp. 299-307.
9. See in this context Collins, Randall 1999 Macro History, Essays in the Sociology of the Long Run, California : Stanford University Press.
10. See Wong, Yoke-Sum 2008 "An Introduction", Yoke-Sum Wong and Derek Sayer eds. Twenty Years of Historical Sociology, Vol.2, Challenging the Field, Blackwell Publishing, pp. 5-8.
11. See Jha, Hetukar "Historical Sociology in India", Yogendra Singh ed. Indian Sociology, Vol.1, Emerging Concepts, Structure, and Change, ICSSR Research Surveys and Explorations, New Delhi : Oxford University Press, pp. 20-86.
12. Myrdal, Gunnar 1968 Asian Drama, An Inquiry into the Proverty of Nations, Vol. III, Harmondsworth, Penguin Books, p. 1575.
13. Ibid, p. 1605.
14. Ibid, p. 1606.
15. Ibid, pp. 1606-1607.
16. WHO/UNICEF Sanitation Assessment Report 2004.
17. See "Magnitude of Sanitation Problem at National and Global levels", Sulabh Sanitation Movement, Sulabh International

Social Service Organisation, New Delhi, pp. 42-43.

18. See Report by Parul Pandey, The Times of India, Patna, 22 November, 2013.

19. See Local Actions for Sustainable Development, Water and Sanitation in Asia-Pacific Region, UN-Habitat, ADB, Asia-Pacific Water Forum, p. 95.

20. See Spears, Dean 2013 "The Long and Short of open defecation", The Hindu, Kolkata, March14.

21. Singh Thakur, Santosh 2014 Healing Touch, Patna ; Novelty & Company, p. 50.

22. See Verma, Sefalika 2008 Kist-Kist Jivan (in Maithili), Patna : Shekhar Prakashan, p. 64.

23. See Divya Trivedi's Report : "Call to recognize sanitation as a legal right", The Hindu, Kolkata, March 20, 2013, p. 18.

24. See report, Local Actions for Sustainable Development, Water and Sanitation in Asia-Pacific Region, ADB, Asia-Pacific Water Forum, UN-Habitat.

25. See the report "Thumbnail Portrait of Sulabh", Sulabh Sanitation Movement, New Delhi : Sulabh International Social Service Organisation, p. 5.

26. Myrdal, Gunnar, op cit, p. 1606.

27. Ibid, p. 1607.

28. Lal, Pyare 1950 "Harijan uplift needs greater impetus", The Searchlight, Patna, 27 November, p. 4.

29. See Mukerji, D.P. 1988 "Indian Tradition and Social Change" in T.K. Oommen and Partha N. Mukherjee eds. Indian Sociology : Reflections and Introspection, Bombay : Popular Prakashan, pp. 1-15.

Sanitation and Society in the Colonial Period

Material regarding people's habit and attitude towards sanitation is not generally available in the records/books produced by the native scholars or observers. However, there are some proverbs existing in the oral tradition of people (loka) which throw much light on their habits and practices. A few of them are described here for example. There is a proverb[1] : "Aangan Bahaarilan Duarey Ghoor Laayilan, Bare, Bare Lenr Pichhuari Giraayilan". This describes women's practice of depositing all the dirt of the house in its front and defecating in the backside (of her house). There is another proverb that reveals the mentality of the people concerning sanitation. According to this proverb[2], "Chal Chalanti, Hag Bharanti, Je Rahanti Se Pochhanti". While going on a long journey, one discharges excreta and urine where he takes rest and departs leaving it to be cleaned by those who would come afterwards. There is one proverb relating to the impact of poor environment on public health. This proverb[3], "Jahar Khaain Na Maahur Khain, Chalal Chalal Sargujaa Jaain" (why should one take any poison for ending his life ? He should simply go to Sarguja.). The explanatory note given in this context indicates that people were aware of the unhealthy environment of some places such as Sarguja (Chhatisgarh), Purnia (Bihar), etc., and the proverb was used to warn those going to such places of what might happen[4]. There is another proverb[5], "Laalaaji Tor Batiyaa Kahi Deb" (Lalaji – I will reveal your secret). Following is the note explaining this proverb[6] : "one day, a Lalaji (a rich man) was eating berries while discharging excreta in an open field. That very day in a wedding ceremony in the village, a female dancer began singing a song, "Lalaji Tor Batiya Kahi Deb..." Lalaji was also present there and as he heard the song he thought that the dancer had seen him eating while discharging excreta and through her song she had started giving hint of her intention of making his secret (eating while defecating) known to people. So, in order to save his face, he paid her lavishly considering that she would be satisfied and would not reveal his secret. But, the dancer thought that her song had been very much appreciated by Lalaji and, therefore, she kept on repeating the song and Lalaji continued to give her reward. However, eventually, he became fed up with his exploitation and, so, he told her to better announce that she had seen him eating berries while discharging excreta". In fact, Lalaji was afraid of being condemned in society for eating while defecating. The proverb, however, indicates it clearly that the practice of going out for discharging excreta prevailed among both rich and poor sections of society. It may also be noted here that in the biographical account of one, Hit Narain Singh, of village Taranpur (Patna), who died in 1866, Ram Din Singh describes an incident that occurred at Danapur (Patna) which clearly implies that defecation in the open was thought to be an unquestionable practice/habit of people in our society[7].

Besides, the association of particular caste group(s) with the job of sweeping and removing human excreta, it seems, was quite visible in the nineteenth century. G.A. Grierson in his famous work, Bihar Peasant Life (1885) refers to pawani / pasari (that is jajmani) system prevailing in the village world that included sweeper (mihtar, hari) caste groups as receiving perquisites annually from their jajmans (patrons)[8]. The conditions of sanitation began to be increasingly considered as an important issue of observation and discussion by the 'outsiders' (British authorities, travellers, journalists, etc.). Most of their observations are recorded in their reports / journals / books, quite a lot of which is now available in print. It appears to be quite necessary to describe this context, one may cite the observation of William Hodges who visited India during the early 1780s. He took note of[9] "A surprising spirit of cleanliness.. among the Hindus" in Bengal and found "the streets of their villages... (being) commonly swept and watered and sand... (being) frequently strewed before the doors of houses". Hodges, it seems, recorded his impression while travelling in Bengal in the last quarter of the eighteenth century for selecting the sites for painting. The reports of the surveys of villages and towns conducted by British authorities since the beginning of the nineteenth century, however, contain much more information regarding the state of sanitation. For example, one may look into the Reports and Diaries (Journals) of Francis Buchanan.

Soon after the end of the eighteenth century, Francis Buchanan at the instance of East India Company government surveyed Mysore and the territories acquired after the Fourth Mysore War and collected information regarding technology, historic sites, castes and their occupations, etc., and his reports (in three volumes) were published in 1807 (London : Cadell and Davies). Then, in 1807 he was directed by the then Governor – General in Council to survey the districts under the Presidency of Bengal. He began the survey of the district of Purnia and completed it during 1809-10. The survey of Bhagalpur district was done during 1810-11, that of the district of Patna and Bihar (Gaya) in 1811-12 and, then, the district of Shahabad was surveyed during 1812-13. Besides, he also covered the districts of Dinajpur, Rangopur and the northern part of the dictrict of Gorakhpur (in U.P.)[10]. In his surveys, he collected details of the conditions and manners of everyday life of people, their education, religion, sects, castes, occupations, etc. He also maintained diaries (entitled journals) of his field work and recorded the details of how he travelled from village to village, how he collected various kinds of information and also how he conducted his observation. His Reports and

Journals are widely considered to be very valuable sources of historical as well as sociological / anthropological studies. Therefore, it appears to be necessary to discuss his field – view account of the caste groups of sweepers / scavengers and sanitary / insanitary conditions prevailing in the villages and towns at that time.

In the district of Purnia, according to him[11] "The tribe of sweepers or scavengers among the Bangalese is called Hari; in the Hindi dialect the same name is also proper, but the Muslim name Hulalkhor, or purifiers, is in more general use. In Matsya, where the tribe Bhumi-Mali, alleged to be the same with the Haris, is much more numerous than towards the west; they have separated into two classes, the Barabhaga... and the Chhotabhaga... All the Haris and Hulalkhors in the western parts are sweepers and together with the Chhotabhaga of Bengal were reported at between five and six hundred families... some have become Miuslims.." Thus, Haris, Hulalkhors and Chhotabhaga Bhumi-Malis were identified as sweepers/scavengers in Purnia. The Barabhaga Bhumi-Malis were not scavengers. Perhaps, due to some serious socio-economic problems, the Chhotabhaga Bhumi-Malis had to take up scavenging for their existence. Besides, it may be noted that the strength of their total population was very limited (between five and six hundred families) in the whole district. This figure may not be very accurate, but, it definitely indicates that population-wise they had negligible space in society. Buchanan also throws light on the question of purity-pollution while narrating the living conditions of people. He wrote[12] : "... there is no space between the fences (of the houses), except holes into which all filthiness and even dead carcases are thrown. So negligent in this point are the natives that, while writing this, I am assured by a gentleman that he this day saw the dead body of a woman rotting in one of these holes. ... maxims of Hindu purity... prevented anyone from touching the body" (emphasis added).

Buchanan took note of complete neglect of the concern for environmental cleanliness among people in general (excluding sweeper and scavenger castes), perhaps, due to dharmashastriya maxims related to purity-pollution. In the large urban centre, Kolkata, he found sweepers being called Mehtar and Mehtarani. In this context, he wrote[13] "The Torahas are a low tribe who chiefly retail fish, but the greater part have been converted to the Moslem faith. Their chief... called Mehtar and.. the female.. Mehtarani... that in Calcutta are applied to sweepers". It seems, as Buchanan's findings in the beginning of colonial era indicate, that the occupation of sweeping/scavenging was not everywhere followed by any one particular caste group; different castes or sections of castes in different places / regions took it up most probably to ensure their survival.

In the districts of Patna and Gaya, he found 200 houses of sweepers and scavengers[14]. About them, he mentions that[15] "The sweepers and scavengers are the lowest of all tribes, and in the Hindi dialect of this district are called Hulalkhor. Some have become Muhammadans without escaping from their degradation,..." Regarding villages, he recorded his observation in the following words[16] : "The villages, as usual... are built of mud, and the houses closely huddled together, so as to render a passage through them... always difficult, and often impracticable. This is done... to keep persons of rank from approaching their women; as in former times violence to any pretty girl that was seen, was not uncommon. The huts are naked and mean and the narrow passages are very slovenly, so that the villages are disgusting" (emphasis added). It seems that historical conditions forced the villagers to adopt a particular pattern of housing arrangement in order to ensure the security of women. However, such an arrangement proved to be degrading the environment and their villages eventually became "disgusting". Buchanan also took note of the environmental factor causing disease in society. For example, in the district of Bhagalpur, he found people living on the Man river liable to different chronic swellings[17]. He wrote in this context that[18] "... a neighbouring zamindar dug there a fine well (Indra) which was lined with brick. While this well continued... the discase is said to have appreared in the vicinity less frequently, but since the water has become bad, the disorder has become as common as ever. These circumstances would seem to point out certain condition of the water as the cause of the disease". The necessity of pure drinking water for improving public health was thus clearly pointed out on the basis of field experience. Regarding scavengers, he found them to be of Hari caste and belonging to a section of the large community of Doms, known as Hulalkhors (150 houses) who did not remove the dead bodies[19]. It is important to note that there was another section of Doms who were sweepers and who also removed dead bodies, but did not clean the toilets[20]. So, the occupation of sweeping streets and removing dead bodies was separate from that of cleaning toilets. However, the people engaged in both the occupations were of the same community of Doms, but had practically separated from one another by forming their own subcastes.

In Sahabad[21], he found about 250 houses of "Hulalkhors or sweepers and scavengers". In the town of Sasaram, he observed one Turkish bath (hammam) about which he wrote that[22] "... a man... keep(s) a warm bath and has an endowment... which has probably been continued since the time of Sher Shah. So far as I could learn, he has no employment except when Europeans happen to pass... but this in fact is more than done by most of those who have endowments. Few or none, I presume, avail themselves of the decades following Buchanan's survey. For example, William Taylor visited it around mid-nineteenth century and wrote the following[23]: "Few people know that at Sassaram there is a most excellent hot-both establishment, or "hammam". This formerly appertained to a Mahomedan Charitable Endowment, and was latterly supported by an allowance of fifteen rupees a month. The grant has now been withdrawn, and the proprietors depend on the custom that they get from wretched and dirty travellers" (emphasis added). The town of Sasaram is situated on the highway running from the western part of the country to Bengal since the days of Sher Shah. So, perhaps, endowments were created for the establishment and maintenance of hammam for travellers. However, it seems that those who established endowments and those who maintained hammam had at least some concern for hygiene. Besides, Buchanan found forts (small and big) having separate apartments with baths for the use of women[24]. But, towns / cities were,perhaps, in a hopeless state. In this context, his observation of the conditions of Patna, one of the most important cities of north India, may be cited here. According to him[25] "... (The) predilection for the city would be hard to explain... The street, when it breaks sloughs, is occasionally repaired with earth thrown in by the convicts, the others are left to nature by the police, and the neighbours are too discordant to think of uniting to perform any work. Paving, cleaning and lighting, considered so essential in every European town... are totally out of the question..." (emphasis added). People's indifference to sanitation, it seems, characterized not only rural but also urban areas. In the rural areas, he observed a sort of crisis of drinking water as most of the tanks were dirty having muddy water and the use of such water for drinking was, according to him, the cause of several diseases[26]. Besides, his account of one, Dewai Raja, throws significant light on wrote that[27] "... (In the area of Kharagpur estate) I... came to the south-west corner of the fort of Dewai Raja... Dewai by the Hindus, is supposed to have been of the low tribes called Chandal... but on account of his power, his family have been received within the limits of purity.. They pretend to trace their origin from a Chandal..." Buchanan was informed by a zamindar of Mandar (Bhagalpur) that the whole of Bhagalpur and Kharagpur areas used to be ruled by such rajas (chiefs) till late in the medieval period[28]. Besides, it may also be noted here in this context that in the areas of Punjab in the eighteenth century, scavengers and leather – dressers were quite numerous among the Sikhs, and, further according to William Irvine[29] "In all the parganas occupied by the Sikhs... A low scavenger or leather – dresser, the lowest of the low in Indian estimation, had only to leave home and join Guru, when in a short space of time he would return to his birth-place as its ruler, with his order of appointment in his hand. As soon as he set foot within the boundaries, the well-born and wealthy went out to greet him and escort him home. Arrived there, they stood before him with joined palms awaiting his order... (emphasis added).

One may, under the circumstances, consider it to be reasonable that untouchability was more a result of the game of political power than that of the injunction of dharma shastras. Further, Buchanan's field experience makes it clear that there was not one caste that could be identified as the only scavenger caste even in the region surveyed by him. One may reasonably assume that different caste groups or parts of some caste groups might have joined the profession of scavenging in different periods when they had to confront the crisis of their survival. Crisis-ridden groups might have had no choice other than surrendering to the force of power holders and accepting the notion of their being impure as defined by the power controlling section.

managed to escape from the injunctions of dharma shastra.

However, under the aegis of colonial power, brahmanic orthodoxy came to occupy hegemonic status and, accordingly, castes along with their respective positions and functions based on the injunctions of dharma shastra (which prescribed the practice of untouchability) were considered to be chiefly constituting the social reality in India[30]. After 1857, anthropology, that was virtually a race science dominated by evolutionism, became one of the most important colonial modalities of knowledge and rule, and, consequently, caste increasingly came to be the[31] "primary object of classification and understanding" in the eyes of British authorities. So, various ethnological accounts of castes of different regions were prepared for classifying them according to their racial features, stereotyped images and their positions in caste hierarchy indicated in brahmanic shastras[32]. Thus, the focus of attention of colonial authorities in the second half of the nineteenth century was on the enumeration and description of castes and their conditions in the society at that time. The census operations which began to be conducted in India since 1871-72 were chiefly designed for this purpose[33]. However, in census reports, one finds some important details of the views and findings of census authorities in respect of the castes of scavengers/sweepers.

For example, the first census report of 1871-72, contains the following account in this context[34] : "... the Harees, a scavenger caste, 5,60,000 ; timid but making good steady labourers much sought for work in the indigo factories, 4,30,000 ; the Doms, an impure race employed by the Hindoo to construct the funeral pyres, and remove dead animals and also used as public executioners" (emphasis added). According to this report, the caste of sweepers was different from that of scavengers, most of whom, 4,30,000, were working as labourers in indigo factories. It seems that indigo planters gave them an opportunity of earning by working in conditions more dignified than that of carrying sewage. The 1881-82 census report has a little more elaborate details in this context. According to it[35]. "The Dom caste numbers 721655 of which almost half appear in Bengal, 343,246... In the North-West... the caste is described as basket-making, singing and dancing... socially at the bottom... In some parts, it is a purely scavenger caste, but it is one of the many instances where in one tract of country the place assigned to a caste socially differs from that assigned to it elsewhere. I have been told that while the Dom of Behar is almost an outcast, the same caste in Assam is considered to be quite respectable" (emphasis added). This report indicates it clearly that the status of (even a lower) caste varied from region to region, in one area it was identified as a scavenger caste while in the other (Assam) it had a respectable position. Buchanan's observation in respect of Dewai family (described before), the above mentioned account of Dom, and the assumption of power by Sikh scavengers (mentioned before), it seems, indicate it clearly that the status and occupation of a caste depended more on its socio-economic conditions in a particular society at a particular time than on dharmashastras.

In the said report, the Chuhras of Punjab are mentioned as a scavenger caste[36], the members of which[37] "are to remove unclean substances and to maintain an affectation of sanitation..." (emphasis added). Province-wise strength of this caste has also been given in this report that seems to suggest that their demographic condition was, perhaps, as poor as their socio-economic situation[38]. The 1891-92 census report mentions it clearly that in the country as a whole the number of scavengers was only 139 per 10,000 population[39]. Those who were supposed to "maintain an affectation of sanitation", were, it seems, too few in number to do so to any

This report refers to Pariah, a Tamil caste, having more or less the same position as the one held by Mahars (of the Deccan) and Doms[40]. However, the occupation of Doms was found to be varying from region to region, who were[41] "Mehtar or Bhangi.. in Hindustan and Western India.. In the Punjab, the Chuhra takes.. (Bhangi's) place". Scavengers were identified[42] as "hereditarily dirty and often a foulfeeding crew..", and, therefore, perhaps, were among the first-top four caste groups having infirmity. The following table shows the proportion of afflicted persons per 100,000 of each sex in the caste group of scavengers[43].

Table – 1

Kinds of infirmity	No. per 100,000 males	No. per 100,000 females
Deaf Mutism	110	78
Blindness	281	310
Lepers	95	39

In the 1901-02 census report, some causes of infirmity are discussed in the following words[44] : "The conditions which may conceivably cause or predispose to infirmity must fall under one or other of three heads, viz, locality (including climate), social practices, physical ailments and race. The close connection between cretinism, goiter and deaf-dumbness... is markedly influenced by the water supply, and that it is most common along the course of certain rivers... Social practices – taking ganja and spirits, consanguineous marriages and enforced widowhood... None of these is supported by statistical figures collected... Race and insanity correlation is also proved false... The connection of deaf – mutism with cretinism and goiter has.. been noticed, and all these maladies have been assigned, with apparent reason, to the injurious properties of the water of certain rivers, especially those which flow from the Himalayas, such as the Chenab, the Gandak and the Makhna... Mr. Burn in the United Provinces points out that the infirmity is chiefly found on the new alluvium deposited by the Ghagra, Gandak and Rapti..." Thus, much light was thrown on the problems of public health due to people's dependence on contaminated water for drinking. This report refers to the initiative of the then government for improving water-supply and sanitary arrangements in urban areas, and, also, mentions that efforts had begun to be taken to guard against epidemic disease at the fairs and festivals[45].

It seems that as municipalities and district boards began to be established since the 1860s, measures for the improvement of public health and sanitation began to be taken. However, L.S.S. O'Malley wrote the following in this context in the first decade of the last century[46] : "Outside the municipalities proper methods of sanitation are almost unknown. The tendency of the people is towards aggregation..., as in Bengal, they cluster in closely-packed villages, usually consisting of a main street with narrow and ill-ventilated side lanes. The sanitary conditions are extremely primitive, while the apathy of the people and the unwholesome habits to which they are rooted render the task of village sanitation... most difficult. The houses are generally constructed of earth, and even those who can afford to build houses of brick often will not do so, owing to a superstitious belief that brick-built walls tempt the evil eyes... The wells from which the people obtain their drinking water are shamefully neglected... In many instances, they are surrounded by house – drains...", (emphasis added). Stevenson-Moore's observation in this context may also be noted here. According to him[47], "The village sites are... clusters of thatch-roofed, mud-walled houses with extremely insanitary surroundings. Ventilation is unthought of, and the drainage left to its own care. If windows exist, they are made, at any rate in top of the wall, their use for ventilation being thereby... minimized" (emphasis added).

Stevenson-Moore's contention that "ventilation is unthought of" in the houses of rural areas (mentioned above) seems to be corroborated by the account of Ras Bihari Lal Das's efforts (made in the beginning of the twentieth century), for convincing the people of his locality (in the then district of Darbhanga) of the value of having proper ventilation in their houses for the health of all (and particularly of women)[48]. However, in the towns, O'Malley contended that[49] "In the municipalities there is an organized system of conservancy; night soil and other refuse are removed; and steps are taken to protect the sources of water-supply. But none of them (municipalities) have a regular system for the supply of pure water or an adequate scheme of drainage; and like the villages they suffer from crowded and badly aligned blocks of houses intersected by narrow lanes..." (emphasis added). The gazetteers (of different districts) at that time present more or less the same conditions of sanitation in rural as well as urban areas as described above. For example, one may look into the gazetteers of Bhagalpur, Patna, Munger, etc.[50].

Later, after independence a little more attention was paid to the problem of removing heaps of nightsoil and refuse in the towns. For example, by 1962, there were 18 refuse carts, two conservancy lorries, two nightsoil trucks and two tractors with trailors for collecting nightsoil from small lanes and by-lanes at Jharia, and about 102 public latrines[51]. Vaccination and inoculation against small-pox and cholera had begun to be given in fairs and melas[52]. However, hardly any effective measure could be taken for improving the supply of safe drinking water for controlling the diseases and habits as well as manners of living of people in the rural areas. The accounts of Saran, Champaran, Purnia and other districts in their respective gazetteers[53] prepared soon after independence give an idea of the steps taken by the colonial authorities for improving public health and sanitation in both rural and urban areas. Undoubtedly, they established municipalities and district boards in order to advance the quality of life of people. For improving sanitation, the need of the supply of pure drinking water, sewrage, ventilation in the houses, etc., it seems, drew the attention of authorities. However, it is important to note in this context that the plight of scavengers remained practically ignored.

The issue of liberating untouchable castes from the age-old task of scavenging / sweeping was, however, taken up by Gandhi. He began to launch his mission of ending untouchability since 1915 by improving the cultural, educational and social conditions of those caste groups who were placed at the bottom of society and were known as untouchables[54]. The account of his struggle, the efforts of Harijan Sevak Sangha, and the leaders of Congress under his leadership etc., for the uplift of Harijans have been widely covered and applauded and, therefore, it is not necessary to discuss them here. However, it appears to be striking that Gandhi's strategy of breaking the age-old association of the most wretched of the untouchable castes with sweeping the dead bodies and removing the human excreta remained more or less out of focus in the movement for the uplift of Harijans which, however, continued to gain ground even after Gandhi. Pyare Lal, a close associate of Gandhi, wrote in 1950 (soon after the death of Gandhi) that Harijan uplift movement required more impetus and all the disabilities imposed on untouchable castes by customs should be ended. Echoing Gandhi, he denounced scavenging as most undesirable of such disabilities[55], and contended that[56] "Gandhiji was the originator of the idea that today all should become scavengers by choice and the reformers should set the example in this regard. It will no longer be sufficient if we satisfy ourselves by engaging ourselves in symbolic scavenging on a few special occasions during the year" (emphasis added). It seems that Gandhi thought of bringing dignity to the most undignified work and thus removing the notion of pollution and being polluted. He spared no word in denouncing (from the core of his heart) the custom of relegation of scavenging to untouchables. He prescribed the following as "Constructive" work for the villagers[57] : "The very first problem the village worker will solve in its (village's) sanitation. It is the most neglected of all problems that baffle workers and that undermine physical well- being and breed disease. It the worker became a voluntary bhangi.. he would begin by collecting nightsoil and turning it into manure and sweeping village streets. He will tell people how and where they should perform daily functions" (emphasis added). Gandhi gave honour to the work of bhangis and wrote that in his ashram one Brahman boy had been voluntarily working as a bhangi[58]. He asserted that it is necessary for himself and others of his ashram to set example for undertaking sanitation work[59]. Gunnar Myrdal made a significant observation in this context[60] that "Gandhi demonstrated his faith... by himself breaking the taboo against scavenging.." Unfortunately, this spirit of Gandhi could not be inculcated in later years by even those who worked for the amelioration of the conditions of Harijans. Later, after his death, his schemes and plans were generally ignored except that untouchability was abolished by the Constitution[61]. It was, no doubt, a very important legislation against untouchability. But, the battle against undesirable customs and practices has to be fought in the realm of society and culture. Gandhi was one who realized it in unmistakable terms. His bold step of "himself breaking the taboo against scavenging" (mentioned above) was a remarkable strategy of tackling effectively the age old scavenging practice and untouchability at the same time. But, it seems, this strategy of Gandhi was hardly incorporated in the movement pursued by his followers since the 1930s against untouchability. However, a few decades after his death his spirit seems to have inspired some NGOs of the country, such as Sulabh International Social Service Organization, for carrying on his mission of bhangi mukti and abolishing the tradition of untouchability that has been reinforcing the association of some caste groups with the task of scavenging / sweeping.

The issue of liberating untouchable castes from the age-old task of scavenging / sweeping was, however, taken up by Gandhi. He began to launch his mission of ending untouchability since 1915 by improving the cultural, educational and social conditions of those caste groups who were placed at the bottom of society and were known as untouchables[54]. The account of his struggle, the efforts of Harijan Sevak Sangha, and the leaders of Congress under his leadership etc., for the uplift of Harijans have been widely covered and applauded and, therefore, it is not necessary to discuss them here. However, it appears to be striking that Gandhi's strategy of breaking the age-old association of the most wretched of the untouchable castes with sweeping the dead bodies and removing the human excreta remained more or less out of focus in the movement for the uplift of Harijans which, however, continued to gain ground even after Gandhi. Pyre Lal, a close associate of Gandhi, wrote in 1950 (soon after the death of Gandhi) that Harijan uplift movement required more impetus and all the disabilities imposed on untouchable castes by customs should be ended. Echoing Gandhi, he denounced scavenging as most undesirable of such disabilities[55], and contended that[56] "Gandhiji was the originator of the idea that today all should become scavengers by choice and the reformers should set the example in this regard. It will no longer be sufficient if we satisfy ourselves by engaging ourselves in symbolic scavenging on a few special occasions during the year" (emphasis added). It seems that

Gandhi thought of bringing dignity to the most undignified work and thus removing the notion of pollution and being polluted. He spared no word in denouncing (from the core of his heart) the custom of relegation of scavenging to untouchables. He prescribed the following as "Constructive" work for the villagers[57] : "The very first problem the village worker will solve in its (village's) sanitation. It is the most neglected of all problems that baffle workers and that undermine physical well- being and breed disease. It the worker became a voluntary bhangi.. he would begin by collecting nightsoil and turning it into manure and sweeping village streets. He will tell people how and where they should perform daily functions" (emphasis added). Gandhi gave honour to the work of bhangis and wrote that in his ashram one Brahman boy had been voluntarily working as a bhangi[58]. He asserted that it is necessary for himself and others of his ashram to set example for undertaking sanitation work[59]. Gunnar Myrdal made a significant observation in this context[60] that "Gandhi demonstrated his faith... by himself breaking the taboo against scavenging.." Unfortunately, this spirit of Gandhi could not be inculcated in later years by even those who worked for the amelioration of the conditions of Harijans. Later, after his death, his schemes and plans were generally ignored except that untouchability was abolished by the Constitution[61]. It was, no doubt, a very important legislation against untouchability. But, the battle against undesirable customs and practices has to be fought in the realm of society and culture. Gandhi was one who realized it in unmistakable terms. His bold step of "himself breaking the taboo against scavenging" (mentioned above) was a remarkable strategy of tackling effectively the age old scavenging practice and untouchability at the same time. But, it seems, this strategy of Gandhi was hardly incorporated in the movement pursued by his followers since the 1930s against untouchability. However, a few some NGOs of the country, such as Sulabh International Social Service Organization, for carrying on his mission of bhangi mukti and abolishing the tradition of untouchability that has been reinforcing the association of some caste groups with the task of scavenging / sweeping.

Notes :

1. See Kahawat Kosh (Dictionary of Proverbs), Bhuvaneshwar Nath Mishra 'Madhava' and Vikramaditya Mishra eds. Patna : Bihar Rashtra Bhasha Parishad, 1965 (1st edn.), p. 60.
2. Ibid, p. 280.
3. Ibid, p. 329.
4. Ibid.
5. Ibid, p. 704.
6. Ibid (English version of the note by the present author).
7. See Babu Ram Din Singh Rachita Bihar Durpan (in Hindi, Bihar Durpan first published 1881), 1996 Dhirendra Nath Singh ed., Kameshwar Singh Bihar Heritage Series – 1, Darbhanga, Maharajadhiraja Kameshwar Singh Kalyani Foundation (henceforth Kalyani Foundation), pp. 148-149.
8. See Grierson, G.A. 1885 Bihar Peasant Life, Calcutta : The Bengal Secretariat Press, London : Trubner & Co., pp. 315-316.
9. See Gopal, Surendra and Jha, Tejakar eds. Bihar in the eyes of British Travellers and Painters 1780-1850, 2008, Kameshwar Singh Bihar Heritage Series – 12, Darbhanga (Bihar) : Kalyani Foundation, p. 72.
10. See Buchanan – Hamilton Manuscript Collection, London : Oriental India Office Coll. (Microform Index).
11. An Account of the District of Purnea in 1809-10 by Francis Buchanan, Patna : Bihar and Orissa Research Society, 1928, pp. 255-256.
12. Ibid, p. 134.
13. Ibid, p. 242.
14. An Account of the District of Bihar and Patna in 1811-12 by Francis Buchanan, Patna : Bihar and Orissa Research Society, year of publication not known, p. 312.
15. Ibid, p. 351.
16. Ibid, p. 74.
17. An Account of the District of Bhagalpur in 1810-11 by Francis Buchanan, Patna : Bihar and Orissa Research Society, 1939, p. 174.

18. Ibid.

19. Ibid, p. 250.

20. Ibid.

21. An Account of the District of Shahabad in 1812-13 by Francis Buchanan, Patna : Bihar and Orissa Research Society, 1934, p. 211.

22. Ibid, p. 397.

23. Taylor, William, Thirty-Eight Years in India, Vol. II, London : W.H. Allen & Co., 1882, pp. 147-148.

24. See for example Journal of Francis Buchanan Kept During the Survey of the District of Patna and Gaya in 1811-1812, edited with Notes and Introduction by V.H. Jackson, Patna : Government Printing, Bihar and Orissa, 1925, p. 79 (henceforth Patna-Gaya Journal); Journal of Francis Buchanan Kept During the Survey of the District of Shahabad in 1812-13, edited with Notes and Introduction by C.E.A.W. Oldham, Patna: Government Printing, Bihar and Orissa, 1926, pp. 64-65 (henceforth Shahabad Journal).

25. See Patna-Gaya Journal, p. 174.

26. Journal of Francis Buchanan Kept During the Survey of the District of Bhagalpur in 1810-1811, edited with Notes and Introduction by C.E.A.W. Oldham, Patna : Government Printing, Bihar and Orissa, 1930, p. 58.

27. Ibid, p. 10.

28. Ibid, p. 21.

29. Irvine, William 1989 edn. Later Mughals, vol. I, Delhi : Taj Publication, pp. 98-99.

30. See Mukherjee, Ramkrishna, The Dynamics of a Rural Society, Berlin : Akademie-Verlag, 1957, pp. 82-83 ; Dirks, Nicholas B. Castes of Mind, Colonialism and the Making of Modern India, New Delhi : Permanent Black, 2002, p. 14.

31. Dirks, Nicholas B. Castes of Mind, Colonialism and the Making of Modern India, New Delhi : Permanent Black, 2002, p. 45.

32. See Jha, Hetukar, "Historical Sociology in India", Indian Sociology, Vol. 1, Yogendra Singh ed., ICSSR Research Surveys and Explorations, New Delhi : Oxford University Press,

2014, pp. 31-33.

33. Dirks writes in this context that ".. the spirit of caste attained its apotheosis with the census", Dirks, Nicholas B. op cit, p. 48.

34. Memorandum on the Census of British India of 1871-72, Henry, Waterfield, London : George Edward Eyre and William Spottiswoode, 1875, p. 23.

35. Report on the Census of British India of 1881-82, W. Chichele Plowden, London : George Edward Eyre and William Spottiswoode, 1883, p. 286.

36. Ibid.

37. Ibid, p. 297.

38. Ibid, p. 286.

39. Report on the Census of British India of 1891-92, Jervoise Athelstane Bains, London : George Edward Eyre and William Spottiswoode, 1893, p. 190.

40. Ibid, p. 200.

41. Ibid.

42. Ibid, p. 240.

43. Ibid, p. 242.

44. Report on the Census of India of 1901-02, Vol. 1, H.H. Risley and E.A. Gait, Calcutta : Government Printing, 1903, pp. 135-139.

45. Ibid, p. 86.

46. O'Malley, L.S.S., Bengal District Gazetteers, Muzaffarpur, Calcutta : Bengal Secretariat Book Depot, 1907, pp. 45-46.

47. Quoted in O'Malley, L.S.S., op cit, p. 45.

48. See Jha, Hetukar "Introduction", Tirhut in Early Twentieth Century, Mithila Darpan of Ras Bihari Lal Das, Hetukar Jha ed. Kameshwar Singh Bihar Heritage Series – 8, Darbhanga (Bihar) : Kalyani Foundation, 2005, p. VII.

49. O'Malley, L.S.S., op cit, p. 46.

50. Byrne, J., Bengal District Gazetteers, Bhagalpur, Calcutta : Bengal Secretariat Book Depot, 1911 ; O'Malley, L.S.S., Bengal District Gazetteers, Patna, Calcutta, Bengal Secretariat Book Depot, 1907 ; O'Malley, L.S.S., Bengal District Gazetteers, Monghyr (Revised edn.), Patna : Government Printing, Bihar

and Orissa, 1926.

51. Roy Chaudhury, P.C., Bihar District Gazetteers, Dhanbad, Patna : Secretariat Press, 1964, p. 606.

52. Ibid, p. 663.

53. See Roy Chaudhury, P.C., Bihar District Gazetteers, Purnea, Patna : Secretariat Press, 1963 ; Roy Chaudhury, P.C., Bihar District Gazetteers, Saran, Patna : Secretariat Press, 1960 ; Roy Chaudhury, P.C., Bihar District Gazetteers, Champaran, Patna : Secretariat Press, 1960.

54. See Pandey, Braj Kumar, Dalit Samasya Ki Rajniti (in Hindi), Muzaffarpur : Abhidha Prakashan, 2003, pp. 37-47.

55. See Lal, Pyare, The Searchlight, 27 September, 1950, p. 4.

56. Ibid.

57. Harijan, January 9, 1937.

58. Quoted in Pandey, Braj Kumar, op cit, p. 47.

59. Ibid.

60. Myrdal, Gunnar, op cit, p. 1607.

61. See Jaffrelot, Christophe, "The World's Largest Democracy During the Congress System", in Chistophe Jaffrelot ed. India Since 1950, New Delhi : Yatra Books, Foundation Books, 2012, p. 5.

Untouchability and Sanitation in Pre-Modern Era

"On one occasion the Guru (Dharmasvamin, 13th century) having wrapped his alm's bowl in a piece of cloth, decided to ford a river (near Nalanda or Gaya), instead of taking a longer circuitous route. He was carried away by the current towards the opposite bank but noticed a man of dark complexion standing on the bank and shouted to him "save me from the river" ! The man shouted back "I am of low Caste", and did not help him". (Biography of Dharmasvamin, A Tibetan Monk Pilgrim, Original Tibetan Text Deciphered and translated (into English) by George Roerich, with a historical and critical Introduction by A.S. Altekar, Patna : K.P. Jayaswal Research Institute, 1959, p. 85).

"(In Bettiah, the headquarters of the district of West Champaran, Bihar in 1968) A bull charged towards a young boy in the market place. At first, several people rushed forward to rescue him. Then someone shouted, "This boy is from the scavenger colony" ! And suddenly the crowd dispersed" (An eye-witness account of Bindeshwar Pathak, quoted in Rashmi Bansal, I have a Dream, New Delhi : Westland Ltd., 2011, p. 11).

Both of the above mentioned field-view accounts, one of the thirteenth century and the other of the twentieth century (after independence when the practice of untouchability has been banned by law) apparently indicate that the notion of untouchability was so deeply entrenched in the minds of lower as well as upper caste men that they had virtually no consideration even for the most important human obligation of saving one's life. However, there seems to be an important difference between the two to easy to explain the second (twentieth century) account in terms of the brahmanical tradition upholding the norms of untouchability, it is difficult to understand the behaviour of the man who refused to help Dharmasvamin saying simply that he was of "low caste". Could it be supposed that brahmanical rules dominated those of "low caste" to such an extent that the man (belonging to this caste) did not afford courage to rescue Dharmasvamin? It is difficult to accept this assumption in the light of the fact that before the nineteenth century, there prevailed a number of visibly significant religio-social traditions (such as Vaishnava, Shaiva, Shakta, various Tantric cults, etc.) including that of Brahmanism as well commanding the world-views of different sections of people in India. Therefore, the question of brahmanical hegemony over the entire Hindu world can hardly ever be considered[1]. However, Friedhelm Hardy's view seems to be reasonable in the context of understanding the mentality of the "low caste" man who refused to oblige Dharmasvamin. Hardy analysed the life-story of one, Muli, an untouchable belonging to Orissa on the basis of the study (of Muli's life-story) conducted by J.M. Freeman, an American anthropologist[2]. Hardy refers to the following incident in the life of Muli[3]: "Muli manages to acquire a small piece of land. But eventually a Brahmin cheats him out of it. It comes to a court case. When it is obvious to all officials that Muli has indeed been wronged, the Brahmin challenges him ; if you are indeed telling the truth, then touch me ! Muli cannot do so, and loses the case. Why should this have happened, this inability to accept the challenge and touch the brahmin ? I untouchable… Either side represents a grave threat and danger to the other.. This is applicable to both extremes on the scale of… (caste) hierarchies : 'pollution' in the sense of the Dharmashastra would be merely a one sided relationship" (emphasis added).

In the light of Hardy's interpretation, one may consider the response of the "low caste" man to the call of Dharmasvamin as based in the former's belief that he would also lose his caste or would be condemned/punished by his caste men for violating his caste norm of keeping the followers of pollution principle at a distance. This assumption seems to be supported by the fact that since the ancient period the relationship between upper varnas (following Vedic/brahmanical tradition) and shudras (including untouchable castes) following non-Vedic or even anti Vedic traditions, was visibly characterized by conflict. The latter category was a broad one following Lokayata (Tantrism). According to Debiprasad Chattopadhyaya[4], "… competent scholars have conjectured that (Tantrism) could have been even older than the Vedas. (it) was… distinctly non-Vedic and… opposed to the Vedic tradition… Tantrism was… lokesu ayatah, prevalent among people (loka)… the (Tantras) have practically superceded the Vedas, over a large part of India". Lokayata and Tantrism were the same[5]. Loka had their own tradition which had nothing to do with dharmashastras, that is, Vedic tradition[6]. Hajari Prasad Dwivedi also held the view that Loka category included all the people who did not depend on dharmashastras[7]. Lokayata (Tantras) was opposed to varna-ashram principle and did not have any space for jati/varna. It simply recognized individual irrespective of his/her sex, caste/varna, etc. According to Debiprasad Chattopadhyaya, there was a number of sects and[8] "There was… no real dearth of sectarian rivalry". Sectarian rivalry, however, continued to prevail among people[9] Vidyapati in the fifteenth century described the situation in the following words[10]: "There be several kinds of heretics... such as Buddists,.. Charvaka (Lokayatikas) etc... Enemies are they of the Vedas, while men versed in the Vedas are enemies of their beliefs..." Ideological conflict, perhaps, coincided with or contributed to the hostility between the brahmanas and shudras. R.S. Sharma writes in this context that[11] ".. the general tenor of intense hostility between the brahmanas and the sudras... about the third and fourth centuries A.D. is unmistakable. Sometimes it is expressed in religious, and at other times in social and political idioms... sudra antagonism against brahmanas can be explained if we bear in mind that the brahmanas gave the sudras the lowest ritualistic position in order to make them work as slaves,... domestic servants..." It seems that the conflict or antagonism between Brahmans and shudras gradually grew to be visible and sharp as the latter (<u>loka</u>) was ideologically empowered by Tantrism, that[12] ".. provided for the initiation of women and sudras and did not discriminate between the Varnas. Women were some of the greatest exponents of tantrism. Sudra teachers could initiate sudras and Chandalas..." In this context, Debiprasad Chattopadhyaya contends on the basis of his study of several works that[13] "We find... supreme importance being attached in the <u>Tantras</u> to such characters as the Chandali, Dombi, Rajaki, Saavari and others. <u>These are all female names and they represent some of the lowest castes carrying on the most despised occupations</u>... Being thus associated with the despised Castes, Tantrism.. (had) no respect of caste distinction and caste superiority... Indifference towards the caste system was often expressed as open revolt against it" (emphasis added). Revolt against caste system, perhaps, manifested in the conflict of brahmanas and shudras mentioned (before) by R.S.

predominance of Brahmanism began to decline since the rise of Buddhism, Jainism, Lokayata and other religio-cultural cults and sects which gained from time to time political patronage in different areas. Loss of political support to Brahmanism in any region, perhaps, led to the weakening of its control over the ideological forces opposing it. However, Buddhist as well as Jain texts, according to R.S. Sharma, continued to treat untouchability in more or less the same way as that of brahmanical Dharmashastras[14]. But, Tantrism (or Lokayata) remained opposed to Brahmanism and its norms and rules (including untouchability). One may, thus, contend that the practice of untouchability must have remained quite weak in the areas where Lokayata or Tantrism (particularly its Vamachar cults) was popular and had a large following enjoying political support. So, untouchability as a socio-cultural phenomenon may be considered to be varying across space and time depending to a great extent on the variation in the nature of political power. Though the travel reports of Fa-Hsien (5th century A.D.) and Yuan Chwang (7th century A.D.) mention the existence of chandalas, pariahs, scavengers and a few other castes in a way that implies the prevalence of untouchability at that time[15], the region-wise variation in its practice is not clear. Such reports have to be revisited for ascertaining whether they are based simply on observation or on what was reported by their knowledgeable informers (possibly Brahmans or Buddhists). It may also be stated here that Al-Biruni's account of the 11th century A.D. which more or less repeats what had been mentioned by Yuan Chwang in the context of untouchable castes, was considered by B.P. Majumdar to have been derived simply from scriptures[16]. However, this view was controverted by Qeyamuddin Ahmad[17]. What appears to be important for consideration is that most of such travel accounts and some generalized picture of the conditions of untouchable caste groups as well as untouchability implying it (untouchability) to be invariable irrespective of the variation in socio-political situation in different regions and different periods. It is difficult to accept the view that any particular practice/custom can remain unchaned in any society for good.

The tales of Katha Sarita Sagar (11th century), which are supposed to reflect on social practices actually followed in society[19] suggest a different view of the chandalas. For example, there is a story that once, long ago, a Brahman and a chandal together decided to pursue the path of renunciation and sat near the river Ganga to do tapasya. Of the two, the latter quite sucussfully controlled his mind and concentrated on his mission while the former (the Brahman) failed to do so[20]. There is another story of the son of a Rajak (Dhobi, an untouchable) who was married to the daughter of a king because the boy had fallen in love with her[21]. According to Padma Velaskar[22], "Shastric Brahmanism reached its pinnacle (in Maharashtra) under Peshwa rule. The asprushyas were considered as severely impure and harsh disabilities were inflicted on them ...". However, in pre-colonial days (in the 17th century), a Jain trader had to stay for a night in a village of "thiefs" (untouchables) on his way to Patna from Agra. He declared himself to be a Brahman by wearing sacred thread. Choudhary, the head of thiefs, gave him proper respect and offered hospitality[23]. The behavior of thiefs with the Jain trader disguised as a Brahman indicates that brahmans had no hesitation in living with untouchables in their houses. In the village schools of Bihar and Bengal, according to William Adam[24], "Parents of good caste.. (did) not hesitate to send their children to schools conducted by teachers of ... the Chandala and other low caste(s)". In Bihar, particularly in Bhojpuri speaking belt, the sacred order of village gods and goddesses (constituting the Lokayata tradition) was very popular and the untouchable castes (particularly Dusadhs) enjoyed its leadership and also held powerful positions of authority in the management of estates[25]. Under the circumstances, the practice of untouchability must have been blunted. Similar instances of variation in untouchability may be gleaned from different sources of history of different regions of the country. However, after all, untouchability as such has visibly existed in our society since ancient period. So, it seems necessary to discuss how and under which socio-economic conditions it appeared and began to be exploited by upper sections for purposes of performing the task of sweeping and removing human excreta.

Dev Raj Chanana, a renowned historian of ancient India, contends in this context on the basis of his study of Pali and Sanskrit texts that[26] "… from the Rigveda upto Kautalya, the dasas are not considered untouchables… But this does not mean that there were no untouchables among them. Certain groups, such as the Chandalas were considered untouchables and were obliged to live outside the town or village. The question of connubiality or commensality with them did not arise. Yet this social 'boycott' did not release them from obligations imposed on them. They were obliged to take up menial jobs, like that of privy-cleaning, of lifting carcasses, etc. Obviously, no one would have volunteered to take to such a profession. This obligation of carrying out dirty jobs was imposed on them by the "touchables" who took care not to remunerate the Chandalaas properly… This is confirmed by the description of the Chandalaas as the most miserable of human beings, forced to live in whatever way, with whatever little that was given to them, adding to it a little money earned by the sale of birds…" (emphasis added). Chanana makes it clear that the "touchables", that is, Aryas in general, became politically very powerful and degraded some of the groups belonging to 'dasa' category by creating a section of "untouchables" among them. A few of the untouchable caste groups such as Chandalas were forced to take up menial jobs for serving the upper varnas and live a wretched life due to the contemptuous attitude of the dominant group toward them. How and when did this trend emerge in ancient period? According to Vivekanand Jha, a section of society had become identified as untouchable by circa A.D. 200[27]. From Rigvedic time to c.200 A.D. there is a long period in which the society was subjected to a lot of pressure and conflict of different groups. Prabhati Mukherjee on the basis of her study of Vedic, later Vedic, Buddhist and other relevant Sanskrit texts, contends that Aryas (Rigvedic people) had inimical relationship with Dasas/Dasyus, Rakshasas, Asuras, etc.[28], who, it seems, did not subscribe to Vedic ideology. Besides, there were also people of some regions such as Kikat (south Bihar or Haryana)[29] "who were un-Aryan, atheists (according to Aryas' view) and did not perform yajna... These people resisted... domination (of Aryas), and hence Indra was urged to grab their wealth". The Rigvedic people, according to her[30], "nursed an antipathy to Dasas, Rakshas, Asuras and Panis. These people, except the Dasas, were constantly being driven out of their homes and hearths, because they spoke a different language and did not follow the religion of the Aryas... The people of Kikata were hated, because they were anti-Agni and anti-sacrifice... Ritual condemnation of Chandala became clearer in the Upanishads" (emphasis added). The untouchability aspect of some caste groups, according to her, began to be visible since the composition of the Sutra literature (800 B.C.)[31]. It seems that before the 6th century B.C. the society was polarized primarily between the Aryas and others who did not accept the authority of the Vedas. However, according to Mukherjee[32], ".. the balance of power gradually turned in their (Aryas') favour" which, perhaps, made it authority of the Vedas as 'untouchables' and forced them to do jobs which they considered unclean or degrading. For example, according to Vaikhanas-Smarta-Sutra, Chandalas were engaged in cleaning filth from streets and other places[33]. Thus, it seems, the growth of political and economic power in favour of Brahmanism facilitated its politico-ideological strategy to hold 'others' (non-Aryas) in contempt. The language of contempt was based on the concept of ashuchi (unclean). What was thought to be ashuchi was not to be touched in order to escape physical as well as spiritual pollution. Since the domain of the spiritual was considered to be rooted in that of the physical not only by Lokayata but also by Nyaya-Vaisheshika and Sankhya philosophies at that (later Vedic) time[34], the attitude to non-Aryas, perceived to be ashuchi by the Aryas, perhaps, became, legitimized and more severe. So, an ashuchi person became asprishya (untouchable) from religions point of view. Untouchability thus seems to have been sanctified by Brahmanism and this sanctification was later explicitly or implicitly upheld by Buddhism and Jainism (discussed before). Perhaps, the growing needs of society also contributed to it. Mukherjee points out that urban settlements in particular required the services of such people[35]. This view has been proposed by others as well[36]. The phase of second urbanization began in India since the 6th century B.C. and this might have induced the dominant groups to utilize the labour of untouchables for cleaning their latrines, urinals, streets, etc., in their towns. Possibly, the association of Chamars, Doms or Chandals (Bhangis), etc., with sanitary functions was forged in this period and this association continued to be practised in the course of the rise of urbanization in later centuries.

Here, it will not be out of place to discuss, at least briefly, the background of the rise of urbanization and the beginning of Buddhism and Jainism. According to Radhakrishna Choudhary[37], "By the sixth century B.C., artisans, craftsmen, traders, financiers, etc., assumed unprecedented importance and followed their lucrative professions with great proficiency, profit and affluence... The rise of urban commercial classes... The setthis helped the growth of urban life. The emergence of urban commercial economy was due to the development of iron technology". However, Chaudhary further contends in this context on the basis of his study of Buddhist and Jain texts (such as Dighanikaya, Anguttaranikaya, etc.) that[38] "By playing into the hands of the commercial classes, Jainism and Buddhism obscured the class consciousness of the masses and kept them in subjection... Jainism and Buddhism deprecated the profession of sickle and yoke and branded the cultivators as engaged in a mean and violent work and in their scale of values the labourers ranked with slaves" (emphasis added). Class consciousness of the masses of ancient days may be supposed to refer to the consciousness of ethnic identities and traditions of different groups constituting the masses at that time. Their identities and traditions were not only ignored but "deprecated" and they were held "in subjection". Consequently, perhaps, they were "engaged in a mean and violent work". Doing "mean work" implies not only doing cultivation but engaging in all sorts of jobs of sweeping, cleaning, scavenging, etc. The trends of Buddhist and Jain policies, thus, also seem to have contributed to the association of some of the subjugated (untouchable) groups with the "mean work" of sweeping, scavenging, etc.

However, the cities/towns were established at that time on the basis of a very well-charted plan. For example, one finds the details given in this context in the Arthashastra of Kautilya[39]. The plan includes an authority structure having well – organized hierarchy of positions, each position having well –

defined roles. The mayor of the city was called nagaraka who had the duty of inspecting water supply, road condition, city's space, subterranean passage and city's defence[40]. He had a number of subordinates to look after different functions and arrangements concerning sanitation, housing sites, prevention of crime, etc.[41]. It is not necessary to deal with the details of this plan here. However, it seems apparent that much attention was paid to keep the physical environment of the city quite clean, arrange for the safe water supply and consider the need of latrines, urinals, scavenging, etc., seriously. The account of Megasthenes indicates that the plan of Arthashastra was to a great extent implemented in Pataliputra[42]. Besides, Satyendra Kumar Jha, a well-known archaeologist, has dealt with the issue of sanitation quite comprehensively on the basis of the archaeological excavations of some of the ancient urban sites. According to him[43], "Sanitary provisions and drinking water facilities were two major municipal requirements that were... given special attention... Ever since the PGW (Painted Grey Ware) phase (12th century B.C. to 6th/5th century B.C.), the pits for the disposal of refuge were contrived. These were simple dug-outs from the earth, so that the refuge may accumulate at one point and one place, rather than litter away and grow around the dwellings. This was.. the first major step towards civic discipline. From the PGW levels at Jakhera, we have evidence of an unlined circular pit... circular pits of varying dimensions have been noticed... With the arrival of the NBP (Northern Black Polished) ware (since 600 B.C.) such pits become almost an inalienable phenomenon of urban waste-disposal system. Most of the major urban sites like Shvavasti, Koushambi, Rajghat (Varanasi), Rajgir.. have yielded such pits" (emphasis added). "Simple dug-outs from the earth" might have been without any shape in the beginning which, gradually, underwent innovation as, were discovered. The first type belonging to the early phase of NBP (600-400 B.C.) was circular of about 60-50 cm in diameter dug out up to the depth of 7.14 m. below the ground level extending beyond the water table so that the excreta could fall directly into the sub-soil water. Care was taken in its construction to prevent it from falling[44]. The second type of pit latrine was more or less same except that its diameter was larger and it went up to the depth of only 4.36 m.[45]. Further, terracotta rings, encased in tiers, were introduced into circular pits. The ring-well finds cover a wide area from Shahbazgarhi in north to Arikamedu in south and Brahmanabad in west to Mahasthanagarh in east, but, according to Sankalia, it was first brought into use around 6-5th century B.C. in the Ganga Valley[46]. Considering it to be a major innovation, Jha writes that[47] "One of the major utilities of terracotta ring – well was in the form of latrines. The incessantly growing pressure of population and need for permanence of the latrine devices necessitated the technique of terracotta rings to be applied for latrines. The terracotta encasing would allow deeper cut into the earth, would provide permanence to pits... It would also mean least contamination of the adjoining region. These latrines with deep cuttings into the earth would also mean the absence of odour and minimal health hazard... One of the major advantages of its application was that it would provide a relatively permanent choice for inside toilet, as outside toilet would become increasingly difficult to utilize due to the constant expansion of the town area and consequential shrinking (of) waste lands..." (emphasis added). It seems that since the 6th-5th century B.C. urbanization grew quite visibly and simultaneously pressure of population in town/city areas might be increasing substantially. As a result, having toilet inside one's dwelling place might have been considered quite necessary for a large number of people.

required its cleaning regularly for which the houseowner, perhaps, found it easy to utilize the labour of any family belonging to the bottom (untouchable) layer. Thus, it seems, the association of some untouchable caste groups with cleaning/sweeping filth etc., began to be practised as a constituent of inter-family network, which, possibly, contributed a great deal to the institutionalization of the identity and status of scavengers.

The drainage system was quite well developed in ancient cities. The archaeological findings indicate that[48] "The dimensions of the burnt – brick drains at Hastinapur and Kaushambi suggest that they were meant to drain out sewage or rain water from... the city. The burnt – brick drains of smaller dimensions were to carry off waste – water from individual houses... Such drainage devices have been reported from Hastinapur, Kaushambi, Mathura, Rajghat, etc." The drainage device at Pataliputra was much improved. Archaeological excavation has revealed that[49] "City's major drains were wooden in masonry, huge in dimensions... thoroughly covered... well-equipped to carry away most of the city's sullage and waste-water beyond the palisade-line, and deposit them safely into the moats. The moats beyond and around the city's fortification were well-connected with major rivers like the Ganga and Son... the entire township... (was) well-connected with an extensive network of drains.." At Chirand (Bihar) during the period from 100 B.C. to A.D. 300[50], "The houses were built in a planned manner. Burnt bricks became the chief building material... The exposed residential complex.. (was) fairly large in area. In one of the blocks... two inter-connected rooms were found. A drain ran beneath the floor of the house and terminated in a cistern outside the main building. These rooms were probably used as bathrooms or privies". It appears to be quite clear from archaeological findings that ancient towns/cities were well planned. The residential sites as well as houses, drainage system for sewage disposal, road construction, etc., used to be quite systematically designed[51]. Civic life, it seems, must have been relatively quite healthy and disciplined. However, it is contended by some of the renowned historians that urbanization began to decline after the third century A.D.[52]. Possibly, along with the decline in the number of towns/cities, the role of planning and organizing the different sectors (of city) gradually also lost its value.

For example, one finds in Varna Ratnakara, an early 14th century work, the description of a city that existed at that time in Tirhut (north Bihar). The author, Jyotirishvara, mentions that in the prominent areas of the city there were residential sectors of prostitutes and centres of gambling[53]. Besides, the cremation ground has been depicted as a great centre of Tantric activities[54]. The book describes many activities which throw significant light on the life lived in city/town in the medieval period. However, one does not find even a slight description of sanitary measures mentioned anywhere in the text. Possibly, the arrangement for sewage disposal and getting drinking water had become more dependent on the working of inter-family network.

Tillotson has worked on the social history of mansions (havelis) of north India during Mughal days[55]. Her study throws much light on how drinking water was procured and what was the arrangement for the disposal of waste and excreta. According to her[56], "Every day the water stores of the haveli had to be filled, and where there was no well in the building, water had to be brought from outside. It was carried either by the household servants or by special water-carriers (commonly called bhistis)... When wells became badly polluted, drinking water had to be found from other sources, as the emperor Jahangir observed in seventeenth-century Ahmedabad : '... water (of the wells) is very bad and unpalatable... mostly salt and bitter, and the tanks in the neighbourhood of the city have become like buttermilk from washermen's soap. The upper classes who have some property have made reservoirs in their houses, which they fill with rain water in the rainy season, and they drink that water until the next year'. This seventeenth century account of the emperor, Jahangir, makes it clear that tanks were generally polluted by washermen. Probably, due to the pressure of the need of relatively a large population in the city for getting their clothes cleaned by washermen (untouchables who had to depend on tank water for washing large bundles of clothes) the water of tanks became too polluted to be used for the purpose of drinking. Further, according to Jahangir, the upper class families had made their own arrangement for storing clean water in their houses. But, all those who could not afford to do so, might be depending on polluted water of tanks. The state machinery of the city had, probably, no responsibility in this context. Tillotson writes that each haveli had latrines and every day[57], "the sweeper would come to clean out the haveli latrines. These latrines were often so designed that the waste fell onto a metal tray which could be removed from outside the haveli, but the sweepers had to come into the havelis to clean the latrines themselves... To the Hindus, sweepers were untouchable : their touch was pollution". She refers to John Harrison's study of the sanitary history of Allahabad. There were two forms of latrines in the city houses[58]: "One was built over a deep dry well sunk in the courtyard, where it easily contaminated the family's water supply; the other opened via a shutter and a drain to an uncovered pit outside the house. Sweepers cleaned these latrines from outside via the shutter, but the cesspools formed a source of public infection". Tillotson's account makes it clear that scavengers, sweepers, washermen, etc., had become connected to the community by jajmani relationships[59] forming the inter-family network (which had

So far, the discussion has remained focused on different aspects of the conditions of sanitation chiefly in urban sector since ancient period. As far as the rural areas are concerned, the paucity of sources makes it difficult to discuss any field-view account of past centuries in this context. Besides, it may be mentioned that there might have been relatively little pressure of population on the vast hinterland. In the whole South Asian region, population increased from 70 millions in A.D. 14 to only 79 millions in A.D. 1500[60]. In India, at the time of the death of Mughal emperor, Akbar, W.H. Moreland writes[61] that ".. we are justified in concluding that there must have been... about 100 millions of people.. only one-third of what the same area contained in 1911.." Further, according to him[62], "... there was more forest and less cultivation, we may be sure that... the rural population enjoyed an unrestricted... (access to forest)...", Under the circumstances when jungle was available in abundance around the villages, the practice of defecating in the open might have appeared to be quite convenient to rural people. It seems that this practice was widely prevalent particularly in rural areas since long as one finds norms prescribed in this context in dharmashastra texts of ancient and medieval periods.

Dharmashastra literature is supposed to be of three successive eras according to P.V. Kane : ancient dharmasutras and Manusmriti are traced back to the period[63] "dating from at least the 6th century B.C. to the beginning of the Christian era (first century A.D.). Next comes the period when most of versified Smritis were composed and it ranges from the first centuries of the Christian era to about 800 A.D. The third period is that of commentators and the writers of digests. This covers over a thousand years from about 700 A.D... the general tendency was to write works... in the nature of digests containing a synthesis of all the dicta of Smriti writers...

Ratnakaras of Chandeshvara..." Chandeshvara was a prominent nibandhakara (digest writer) of early 14th century whose work, according to P.V. Kane, exercised much influence over most of the digest writers of Mithila and Bengal[64]. His work, a very comprehensive digest called Ratnakara, is divided into seven books of which the Grihastha Ratnakara[65] "is a very extensive work in 68 tarangas (chapters)... printed in the Bibliotheca Indica Series in 1928". Kamalakrishna Smrtitirtha, who edited the Grihastha Ratnakara, wrote in his "Preface" (in English) to it that[66] "The present treatise is concerned with the enumeration and description of the three-fold duties of a Hindu householder (Grihastha), viz., 1. Civil, 2. Religious and 3. Sanitary... The "sanitary" regulations relate to purification of the body, ... The author has not left untouched a single source..." Since this work, Grihastha Ratnakara, is a very comprehensive compilation of the dicta of various smritikars since ancient period regarding sanitary duties, its chapter on defecation is discussed here in brief.

This chapter (pp. 136-149) is divided into two sections, first deals with defecation (mutrapurishotsarga) (pp. 136-142) and second with ablution (shouch) (pp. 143-149). In the first section, the dicta of the following have been compiled along with the explanatory notes of the author (Chandeshvara) : Manu, Yajnavalkya, Apastamba, Vishnu Purana, Sankhyayana Grihyasutra, Yama, Boudhayana, Vayu Purana, Haarita, Devala, Vashishtha, and Gautama. In the second section (on shouch – ablutions), the regulations suggested by the following have been mentioned : Haarita, Paraskara, Gautama, Apastamba, Devala, Yajnavalkya, Boudhayana, Brahmand Purana, Manu, Daksha, Vishnu Purana, Yama, Shankha, Paithanas, Parijat, Shankha Likhit and Rishyashring. Chandeshvara thus covered a long period from ancient Sutras and Manusmriti (600 B.C. to 100 A.D.) to and 1125 A.D. by P.V. Kane[67]. Photocopies of all the pages of this chapter (of Grihastha Ratnakara) are given on Appendix – A. Appendix – B contains its Hindi translation[68]. Here, it does not seem to be necessary to discuss each dictum separately since all the dicta are given serially on Appendix – A and their translation (Hindi) on Appendix – B. So, only the main thrust of the different dicta are described.

The first section (mutrapurishotsarga) has regulations regarding i. how to defecate, ii. where to do so and iii. the places forbidden from being used for defecation. Here, the main directives are mentioned concerning i., ii and iii :

i. a. One should not utter any sound/word while defecating according to Vishnu, Manu and Haarita.

b. Sankhyayana Grihyasutra, Yama and Manu suggest how to use sacred thread while defecating and in which direction should one discharge urine and excreta.

ii. a. Waste, excrement, urine and dirty water should be thrown at a long distance from one's dwelling place according to Yajnavalkya.

b. Defecation has to be done beyond the boundary of village according to Apastamba.

c. The place should be covered by dry leaves, small shoots of the branches of a tree and small earthen balls or an earthen plate or straw and then one may discharge excreta over it according to Manu.

iii. Combining the dicta of Yama, Haarita, Vashistha and Apastamba, one finds the following places prohibited from being used for defecation : tank/pond, river, waterfall, hilltop, treetop, housetop, mass of dung and ashes, ploughed field, straw, burning wood, human/animal skull, temple premises, cremation ground, roads, crossroads, space of public gathering, village streets, front space of house, garden, arid land, filthy place, mound and the area having crop/vegetation.

It seems clear that some of the dicta are meant for upper varnas since the norms of how to use sacred thread, which direction should be chosen for defecation, etc., have been indicated in them. But, what appears to be quite significant in this context is the concern for keeping the environment (particularly village environment) clean. Roads, crossroads, village streets, temple premises, household space, place of public gathering, etc. had not to be used for defecation. Besides, it seems, care was taken to keep water (for drinking, bathing, etc.) free from pollution. However, there is not a single regulation against defecation in the open.

Part II of this chapter of Grihastha Ratnakara (pp 143-149) deals with ablution after voiding excrement. The dicta of the following are mentioned in this context : Haarita, Paraskara, Gautam, Devala, Yajnavalkya, Boudhayana, Brahmand Purana, Daksha, Manu, Vishnu Purana, Yama, Shankha, Paithanas, Brahma Purana, Parijat and Rishyashringa. Most of the regulations relate to various ways of using water, soil and wooden sticks for ablution. In the context of using wooden sticks, Chandeshvara (the author of Grihastha Ratnakara) comments (p. 144) that the dicta of Smritis had cased to be followed (by the early fourteenth century). However, of all the dicta, the one of Rishyashring appears to be very important. According to him (p. 148), the spot where one does ablution must be cleaned by him ; he cannot get rid of pollution unless the space (where ablution has been done) is thoroughly washed and cleaned by him.

About a century before, Mahamahopadhyaya Ganga Nath Jha, drawing on such ancient works as Charaka – Samhita, Sushruta – Samhita, Matsya – Purana, Agni – Purana, Brihat Samhita of Varaha – mihir, Bhavaprakasha and Vatsyayana's Kamasutra, dealt with the idea and planning regarding sanitation which prevailed in ancient India[69]. According to him[70] sanitation depends on three factors, the way in which towns and villages are planned; the disposition of the dwelling – houses; and the ways of living. He, first, describes the norms of planning the towns and villages in ancient period in the following words[71]: "with every 108 'villages', it was considered necessary to have a 'town'... In both these places, the presence of several roads and public squares was considered necessary; there used to be a large open space in the centre of the town. Within the town, the principal roads were 30 feet wide, and the side – alleys and lanes 8 to 12 feet wide. The village roads were 60 feet wide. The reason for village – roads being wider than town-roads perhaps lay in the fact that, on account of the town being inhabited by well-to-do persons and being infested with all sorts of undesirable men, there was greater danger of theft and robbery in the town than in the village; and this made more compactness desirable. Even at the present day we find people in the villages having their harvesting farms in open spaces away from the dwelling-houses, while in the towns every thing has to be kept within sight. It was this fear... which led the people of the town gradually to concentrate their attention on devising means for safely..." (emphasis added). Archaeological findings also indicate that having toilet inside one's house began to be practised by the residents of towns/cities since 6th-5th century B.C. (discussed before). Ganga Nath Jha's contention that people of the town were gradually led to "concentrate their attention on devising means for safely.." (mentioned above) might have contributed to the said practice of having latrine inside house in the urban areas.

Further, according to Jha[72] "The older Indians paid due attention to drainage. It is laid down that a town or village should always be located upon sloping ground, the slope towards the north and south being considered most desirable; and it was considered very wrong to have ditches and pools in description of cities found in the Ramayana and the Mahabharata that Indian towns in ancient times were clean, houses were placed apart from one another, the roads were clean, wide and well-watered and (occasionally) perfumed; and the markets and squares were carefully distributed (Valmiki's Ramayana, Balakanda). In the Banabhatta also describes the city of Ujjayini as containing wide and clean roads and markets" (emphasis added).

Regarding the disposition of dwelling houses in ancient days he mentions the following directions laid down in the Matsya Purana and the Brihat-Samhita[73]; "No dwelling-house is to be built upon barren land, or upon a plot that is sandy or damp. Special care should be taken in selecting a site, with a view to avoid the contingency of free access of light and air being endangered by the presence of obstructions... It is said that 'if... in the front of the house there happens to be a puddle, there is sorrow in the household; the presence of a well in close proximity to the house brings upon the inmates the disease of epilepsy, and the presence of a drain leads to suffering (Agni-Purana, Adhyaya, 104)... They were not content with only the cleanliness of the upper surface of the site. It is laid down that before a house is built, the whole ground should be dug up – if possible, until a layer of water is reached, but, in any case – not less than 3 feet deep; and every unclean thing should be removed" (emphasis added).

"All the books", according to Jha[74]," insist upon the latrine being aloof from the rest of the dwelling. But even this latrine was meant for the sick and the infirm only. For the man in ordinary health, it was necessary to go out into the open jungles. It is laid down that one should proceed at least so far from his house as would be reached by an arrow shot with ordinary force..." (emphasis added). Thus, it seems that even in the rural areas shastras directed the house holder to have latrine. However, the latrine was not supposed to be inside the house and had to be used by the sick and the infirm. Genearlly, the practice of open defecation was recommended. Perhaps, the availability of open land and jungle around the village at that time (discussed before) was considered to be a facility in the shastras in the context of sanitation. Further, according to shastras, it was considered[75] "desirable to have open spaces around the house; and this compound had two outlets – the principal gate being on the east; a subsidiary one towards the south. All refuse was to go out of the latter gate; and near this gate was also to be the place for lumber and such work as the hewing of wood and the like. The dwelling – house should not be very far from the source of water supply...".

In respect of the ways of living, it is important to note what Charaka – Samhita (Nidan – sthana, Adhyaya, 2) says about drinking water. According to it[76], "...stagnant water is always heavier than flowing water; sea-water should never be drunk; one should never drink water in which there are insects or rotting vegetation; or which smells badly, or water taken from drying tank or well in which only a little water is left... in the Sushruta – samhita... we find elaborate directions in connection with drinking water. For drinking rain – water, collected before it touches the ground is most highly recommended. But even in rain – water a distinction has been made – one kind has been called Saamudraa coming from the ocean... and the other has been called Gaang, 'coming from the Ganga; the following test has been prescribed; when it is raining place a silver vessel filled with white rice in the rain; after a couple of hours if the water changes its colour and acquires some sort of smell, the water should be regarded as coming from the ocean; while if there is no change in the colour of the water and there is no odour of any kind, it should be regarded as coming from the Ganga. During the rainy season, rain-water is the best for drinking; during the autumn, all water recommended, during spring and summer water from wells and springs is considered best. No drinking water should be drawn from a source in which the dead body of an animal has been found, in which leaves, etc. are rotting, in which people bathe… when however good water is not available, one should either thoroughly boil the water, or should put into it a red – hot ball of iron, before it is used for drinking purposes. For the purpose of cleaning water of mud and other things… the putting into it certain substances… a fruitseed called Nirmali, the root of the lotus plant, waterweeds…".

Ganga Nath Jha wrote in the end of his paper that[77] "It is a mere glimpse of this vast and interesting subject… It is an inviting branch of study, and the present writer has written this paper in the hope that some one more competent to deal with the problems… will be induced to take up the study and give to the world the benefit thereof". But, sanitation as an issue of historical/sociological study remained virtually ignored for about a century. It is, however, striking that in ancient period, a fairly large number of works (such as Sutras, Puranas and those of Manu, Yajnavalkya, Gautam, Rishyashring, Vatsyayana, Charaka, Varah-mihir and others, mentioned before) recommended norms and regulations in the context of sanitation. It is a matter of further research for understanding to which extent the shastric precepts were followed in different regions and in different periods. However, one may reasonably assume that at least the norms were available for suggesting how to plan for village and house sites, what precautions to be taken for the arrangement of drinking water, etc., from the points of view of sanitation. But in the works of the later eras, one hardly finds any account taking consideration of sanitation in the changing situations of society and culture. Possibly, as a result of this, one finds the conditions of sanitation declining

Notes :

1. For details in this context, see Jha, Hetukar, "Relevance of Lokayata as an Alternative Hindu Tradition to the Future of Dalits", (292-309), in Sukant K. Chaudhury ed. Ambedkar and Future of Dalits, New Delhi : Serials Publications, pp. 295-300 ; Chattopadhyaya, Debiprasad, Indian Atheism, New Delhi : People's Publishing House, 2012, p. 17.
2. Freeman, J.M., Untouchable – An Indian Life History, London : George Allen and Unwin, 1979.
3. Hardy, Friedhelm, The Religious Culture of India, Power, Love and Wisdom, New Delhi : Cambridge University Press, 1995, pp. 96-97.
4. Chattopadhyaya, Debiprasad, Lokayata, A Study in Ancient Indian Materialism, New Delhi : People's Publishing House (Pvt.) Ltd., 2012, p. 49.
5. Ibid, p. 51.
6. See, in this context, Paranjape, Jaya, "Loka : Itihas, Purana, Mithak" (in Hindi), Piyush Daiya ed. Loka, Udaipur, Bharatiya Loka Kala Mandal, 2002, p. 415.
7. Tiwary, Ram Chandra, "Loka Ke Pratika Aur Unka Paridrishya" (in Hindi) in Piyush Daiya op cit, p. 384.
8. Chattopadhyaya, Debiprasad, Indian Atheism, op cit, p. 17.
9. See Majumdar, B.P. "Religion and Philosophy (550-1200 A.D.), Pauranic Religion-Vaishnavism, Shaivism, etc." (403-501) in Comprehensive History of Bihar, Vol. 1, Part II, B.P. Sinha ed. Patna : K.P. Jayaswal Research Institute, 1974, p. 423..
10. Vidyapati wrote Purush Pariksha (in Sanskrit), which was translated by George A. Grierson in 1935. See The Test of A Man, Being the Purush-Pariksha of Vidyapati Thakkura, English translation by George A. Grierson, London : The Royal Asiatic Society, 1935, pp. 126-127.
11. Sharma, R.S., Early Medieval Indian Society, Kolkata : Orient Longman Limited, p. 54.
12. Ibid, p. 235.
13. Chattopadhyaya, Debiprasad, Lokayata, op cit, pp. 330-331.
14. See Jha, Vivekananda, "Chandala and the Origin of

Untouchability", The Indian Historical Review, Nos. 1-2, Vol. XVIII, July and January 1986-87, fn. 8 ; p. 31.

15. See Fa-Hsien, the Unassuming Pilgrim, Bhikshu Dr. Thich Minh Chan, Patna : Bihar Research Society, 1975, p. 117 ; On Yuan Chwang's Travels in India (A.D. 629-645), Thomas Watters, edited after his death by T.W. Rhys Davids and S.W. Bushell, New Delhi : Low Price Publications, 2004 (reprint), p. 170, p. 178.
16. B.P. Majumdar's view quoted in India by Al-Biruni, Qeyamuddin Ahmad, ed. New Delhi : National Books Trust 1992, pp. 280-281.
17. Ibid, p. 281.
18. See The Ain-i-Akbari, Vol. II, by Abul-Fazl Allami, translated into English by Colonel H.S. Jarrett, corrected and further annotated by Sir Jadunath Sarkar, Delhi : New Taj Office, 1989 (reprinted), pp. 321-322.
19. See Agrawal, Vasudeo Sharan, "Bhumika" (in Hindi), Mahakavi Somadev Bhatta Virachit Katha Saritsagar, Vol. I, Hindi Translation by Kedar Nath Saraswat, Patna : Bihar Rashtrabhasha Parishad, 1997 (reprinted), pp. 5-26 (henceforth Katha Saritsagar).
20. Katha Saritsagar, Pratham Khanda, p. 617.
21. Ibid, Tritiya Khand, p. 337.
22. Velaskar, Padma, "The Politics of Untouchability and Social Change : A Study of the Scheduled Castes of Maharashtra", Journal of Indian School of Political Economy, Vol. XII, Nos. 3 & 4, July-December 2000, p. 474.
23. See Motichand, "Eka Asafal Vyapari Ki Atmakatha" in Nathuram Premi ed. Kavivara Banarasidasa Virachita Ardha Kathanak, Bombay : Hindi Grantha Ratnakara (Pvt.) Ltd., 1970 (reprinted), p. 17, p. 24.
24. See Basu, Ananthnath "Introduction", Reports On the State of Education in Bengal (1835 & 1838) By William Adam, Calcutta : University of Calcutta, 1941, p. xl.
25. For details in this context, see Jha, Hetukar, Social Structures and Alignments, A Study of Rural Bihar, New Delhi : Usha, 1985,

pp. 17-20.

26. Chanana, Dev Raj, Slavery in Ancient India, As Depicted in Pali and Sanskrit Texts, New Delhi : People's Publishing House, pp. 176-177 (note : 3).

27. Jha, Vivekananda, "Stages in the History of Untouchability", The Indian Historical Review, July, Vol. II, No. 1, 1975, p. 31.

28. See Mukherjee, Prabhati, Beyond the Four Varnas, The Untouchables in India, Delhi : Motilal Banarsidass, 1988, pp. 17-20.

29. Ibid, p. 21.

30. Ibid, p. 34, p. 36.

31. Ibid, pp. 40-43.

32. Ibid, p. 23.

33. Ibid, p. 71.

34. See Chattopadhyaya, Debiprasad, What is Living and What is Dead in Indian Philosophy, New Delhi : People's Publishing House, 2010 (reprinted), p. 239, pp. 422-423.

35. Ibid, p. 105, Note 6.

36. For example, See Fuchs, Stepleen, Children of the Hari : A Study of the Nimar Balahis of Madhya Pradesh, Vienna, Verlag Herold, 1950, quoted in Prabhati Mukherjee, op cit, p. 13.

37. Chaudhary, Radhakrishna, "Unbanisation in Ancient India : Trends and Problems" in Vijay Kumar Thakur ed. Towns in Pre-Modern India, Patna : Janaki Prakashan, 1994, p. 10.

38. Ibid, pp. 10-11.

39. See Kangle, R.P. "Preface", The Kautiliya Arthashastra, Part – III, Bombay : University of Bombay, 1965, p. 19.

40. Ibid, p. 19.

41. Ibid, p. 230.

42. Thakur, Vijay Kumar, Urbanisation in Ancient India, New Delhi : Abhinava, 1981, p. 241.

43. Jha, Satyendra Kumar, Beginnings of Urbanization in Early Historic India, A study of the Gangetic plains, Patna : Novelty & Co., 1998, p. 227.

44. Ibid, pp. 227-228.

45. Ibid, p. 228.

46. Ibid, pp. 228-229.

47. Ibid, p. 230.

48. Ibid, p. 233.

49. Ibid, pp. 236-237.

50. Prasad, Kameshwar, "Transition from Rural to Urban Settlement : A case Study of Chirand", in Vijay Kumar Thakur ed. Towns in Pre-Modern India, op cit, p. 68.

51. See Jha, Satyendra Kumar, op cit, pp. 237-239.

52. See Sharma, R.S., Early Medieval Indian Society, A study in Feudalization, Kolkata : Orient Longman, 2001, p. 104, Note 90.

53. See Varna Ratnakara (in Maithili), eds. Anand Mishra and Govinda Jha, Patna : Maithili Academy, 1980, pp. 110-113.

54. Ibid, pp. 129-130.

55. See Tillotson, Sarate, Indian Mansions, A social History of the Haveli, New Delhi : Orient Longman, 1998.

56. Ibid, pp. 41-42.

57. Ibid, p. 43.

58. Ibid, p. 43.

59. Ibid, p. 45.

60. See Grigg, D.B., Agricultural Systems of the World, An Evolutionary Approach, Melbourne : Cambridge University Press, 1996 (reprinted), p. 6, Table 1.

61. Moreland, W.H., India At The Death of Akbar, Delhi : Sunita Publications, 1989 (reprinted), p. 21.

62. Ibid, p. 135.

63. Kane, P.V., History of Dharmashastra, Vol. I, Part I, Poona : Bhandarkar Oriental Research Institute, 1968, p. 545.

64. Kane, P.V., History of Dharmashastra, Vol. I, Part II, Poona : Bhandarkar Oriental Research Institute, 1975, p. 775.

65. Ibid, p. 764.

66. Smrtitirtha, Kamalakrishna, "Preface", Grihastha-Ratnakara, A Treatise on Smrti by Chandeshvara Thakkura, Calcutta : Asiatic Society of Bengal, Bibliotheca Indica Work No. 249, 1928, pp. VI-VII.

67. Kane, P.V., History of Dharmashastra, Vol. I, Part II, op cit, p. 655.

68. The author is grateful to Pt. Shashi Nath Jha, Professor of Vyakarana (grammar), K.S.D.Sanskrit University, who translated the entire Sanskrit text into Hindi.

69. Jha, Ganga Nath "House-building and Sanitation in Ancient India"; The Journal of the Bihar and Orissa Research Society, vol. II, Part II, June, 1916, pp. 135-151.

70. Ibid, p. 136.

71. Ibid, pp. 136-137.

72. Ibid, p. 137.

73. Ibid, pp. 138-139.

74. Ibid, p. 141.

75. Ibid, p. 145.

76. Ibid, pp. 148-150.

77. Ibid, p. 151.

Appendix A

Grihastha Ratnakara (pp. 136-149)

अथ मूत्रपुरीषोत्सर्गः ।

तत्र विष्णुपुराणे--

ततः कल्यं समुत्थाय कुर्यान्मैत्रं नरेश्वर ! ।
नैर्ऋत्यामिषुविक्षेपमतीत्याभ्यधिकं भुवः ।
तिष्ठेन्न च चिरं तत्र न वा किञ्चिदुदीरयेत् ॥

कल्यमुषःकाले मैत्रं विड्विसर्गः, मित्रदेवताकं मैत्रं, तत्-सम्बन्धात् । नैर्ऋत्यां शयनस्थानात् ।

याज्ञवल्क्यः—

दूरादुच्छिष्टविण्मूत्रपादावसेचनं त्यजेत्[1] ।

आपस्तम्बः—

मूत्रपुरीषे कुर्य्याद्दक्षिणां दिशं दक्षिणापरां वा । गत्वेति शेषः । दक्षिणापरां नैर्ऋतीम् ।

अस्तमिते च बहिर्ग्रामादूरादावसथान्मूत्रपुरीषयोः कर्म्म कुर्य्यात् । आवसथाङ्गेश्रात् । आराद्दूरे ।

मनुः—

दूरादावसथान्मूत्रं दूरात् पादावसेचनम् ।
उच्छिष्टान्नं निषेकञ्च दूरादेव समाचरेत् ॥

पादावसेचनं पादप्रक्षालनम् । निषेक उच्छिष्टद्रव्यप्रक्षेपः ।

तथा— तिरस्कृत्योच्चरेत् काष्ठं पत्रं लोष्ठं तृणानि वा ।
नियम्य प्रयतो वाचं संवीताङ्गोऽवगुण्ठितः ॥

काष्ठादिभिर्भूरत आकाद्य इति पूर्व्वखण्डतात्पर्य्यार्थः । उच्चरेत् पुरीषं त्यजेत् । प्रयतः शुचिः, वाचं नियम्येत्यर्थः । सम्वीतं निवीतम् । सम्वीतं मानुषमिति तैत्तिरीयश्रुतेः । तदङ्गं यस्य तथोक्तः । एतच्च दिवस्त्रपक्षे । कर्णासक्तयज्ञोपवीतकः एकवस्त्रत्वपक्षे—शांख्यायनगृह्यम् ॥

यद्येकवस्त्रो यज्ञोपवीतं कर्णे कृत्वा ।

यथा यमः—

यज्ञोपवीतं कृत्वा तु पृष्ठतः कण्ठलम्बितम् ।

१ मूले पादाभ्यां सिचमुत्सृजेत् ।

विण्मूत्रञ्च गृही कुर्य्याद्यदा कर्णे समाहितः ॥

बौधायनः—

शुष्कतृणमयाज्ञिकं काष्ठं लोष्टं वा तिरस्कृत्याहोरात्रयोरुदक्-दक्षिणामुखः । प्रावृत्य शिर उच्चरेदवमेहेत वा ।

अयाज्ञिकं यज्ञोपयुक्तकुशपलाशादिव्यतिरिक्तं, अवमेहेत मूत्रं त्यजेत् ।

विण्मूत्रोत्सर्गं कुर्य्यादित्यनुवृत्तौ वायुपुराणे—

शुष्कैस्तृणैर्वा काष्ठैर्वा पत्रैर्वेणुदलेन वा ।
मृन्मयैर्भाजनैर्वापि अन्तर्धाय वसुन्धराम् ॥

हारीतः—

घ्राणास्ये वेष्टयित्वा मृत्पात्रीं ग्रीवायामासज्य दक्षिणबाहु-पार्श्वे कमण्डलुमादायोत्सृजेत् ।

मृत्पात्रीं मृत्तिकापात्रीमुत्सृजेत् मूत्रपुरीषे इति शेषः ।

मनुः— मूत्रोच्चारसमुत्सर्गं दिवा कुर्य्यादुदङ्मुखः ।
दक्षिणाभिमुखो रात्रौ सन्ध्ययोश्च यथा दिवा ॥

शांख्यायनगृह्यम्—

नादित्याभिमुखो न जघनेन ।

न जघनेनेत्यनेन जघनसम्मुखता यत्र भवति, तत्र न कुर्य्या-दित्यर्थः ।

यमः—

प्रत्यङ्मुखस्तु पूर्वाह्णे पराह्णे प्राङ्मुखस्तथा ।
उदङ्मुखस्तु मध्याह्ने निशायां दक्षिणामुखः ॥

देवलः—

सदैवोदङ्मुखः प्रातः सायाह्ने दक्षिणामुखः ।
विण्मूत्रे विसृजेन्नित्यं सन्ध्यासु परिवर्ज्जयेत् ॥

तत्र चेयं व्यवस्था—

देवलवाक्यबलात्— प्रातःसायंकालयोस्त्रिमुहूर्त्तयोरुदङ्मुखत्वमेवं यमवचनं तदतिरिक्ते पूर्वाह्णे प्रत्यङ्मुखताप्रापकम् ।

मनुः—

छायायामन्धकारे च रात्रावहनि वा द्विजः ।
यथासुखमुखः कुर्य्यात् प्राणबाधाभयेषु च ॥

छायान्धकारयोः प्राणपीडायां व्याघ्रादिभये च दिङ्मुखनियमो नादर्त्तव्य इति ।

तथा तत्रैव—

न मूत्रं पथि कुर्व्वीत न भस्मनि न गोव्रजे ।
न फालकृष्टे न जले न चित्यां[1] न च पर्व्वते ॥

मूत्रशब्दोऽत्र मलत्यागार्थे लक्षणया पुरीषस्याप्युपलक्षकम् । चित्यामग्निचयनस्थाने चितायां वा ।

तथा—

न जीर्णदेवायतने न वल्मीके कदाचन ।
न ससत्त्वेषु गर्त्तेषु न गच्छन्नपि च स्थितः ॥
न नदीतीरमासाद्य न च पर्व्वतमस्तके ।
वाय्वग्निविप्रानादित्यमपः पश्यंस्तथैव च ॥

---

१ (ख) चितायां ।

न कदाचन कुर्व्वीत विण्मूत्रस्य विसर्ज्जनम् ॥

न पर्व्वत इति पूर्व्ववचनादेव पर्व्वतनिषेधे सिद्धे मस्तकनिषेधो भूयस्त्वाय। यच्च पर्व्वतेष्ववशको परीहारस्तत्रापि मस्तकवर्ज्जनार्थ-मिति पारिजातः। वाय्वादिकं पश्यन् सम्मुखमुपलभ्यमानः।

हारीतः—

न चत्वरोपद्वारयोर्मूत्रपुरीषे कुर्य्यात्, न तीर्थे, न शस्यसम्पूर्णे, न यज्ञभूमौ न यज्ञियानां वृक्षाणामधस्तात्।

चत्वरं नानाजनावस्थानदेशः। काकादिबलिस्थानमित्यपरे। उपद्वारं द्वारसमीपं, तीर्थं पुण्यदेशः, जलावतरणमार्ग इत्येके।

देवलः—

वापी-कूप-नदी-गोष्ठ-चैत्यावासेषु चाम्भसि[१]।
अग्नौ कांस्ये श्मशाने वा विण्मूत्रं न समाचरेत् ॥

वाप्यादिपदं निरुदकभागपरमम्भसः पृथगुपादानात्। चैत्यो ग्रामव्यपदेशको वृक्षः, आवासो वासकरणीयदेशः।

यमः—

पल्वलानि तड़ागानि नदी-प्रस्रवणानि च।
नग-गोमय-भस्मानि फालकृष्टञ्च वर्ज्जयेत् ॥

पल्वलमल्पसरः। तड़ागं कृत्रिमं सरः।

तुषाङ्गारकपालानि देवतायतनानि च।
राजमार्गश्मशानानि क्षेत्राणि च खलानि च ॥
उपवद्धो न सेवेत छायां पश्यंश्चतुष्पथम्।

१ (ख) न बहिर्द्वारोपद्वारयोः   २. मूले चैत्याम्भः पथि भस्मसु।

उदकञ्चोदकान्तञ्च पन्थानञ्च विवर्ज्जयेत् ॥

वर्ज्जयेद्धृत्तमूलानि चैत्यश्वभ्रविलानि च।

उपरुद्धो विन्मूत्राभ्यां पीड़ितो न सेवेत मूत्रपुरीषोत्सर्गार्थमिति शेषः। पन्थानं विवर्ज्जयेदित्युक्तापि राजमार्ग-चतुष्पथ-ग्रहणं दोषातिशयार्थं। श्वभ्रं विदीर्णभूभागः।

वशिष्ठः—

नोप्ते न शाद्वलोपजीव्यच्छायासु।

शाद्वलो हरितस्निग्धो भूभागः।

नोषरे न पराङ्मुखौ नोद्याने नोदकपिण्डयोर्वाकाशे।

नाट्टालस्थित इत्यर्थः।

तथा—

न प्रत्यगनिलेन्द्वर्क-स्त्रीगुरुब्राह्मणाश्चैवावगुण्ठितशिराः।

आपस्तम्बः—

छायायां मूत्रपुरीषयोः कर्म्म वर्ज्जयेत्। स्वां तु अवमेहेत।

स्वीयछायां प्रतीति शेषः। तेन स्वच्छायायां मेहने न दोषः।

तथा तत्रैवः—

न सोपानत्को मूत्रपुरीषे कुर्य्यात्।

तथा तत्रैव—

गोदेवताभिमुखो मूत्रपुरीषयोः कर्म्म वर्ज्जयेत्।

गौतमः—

न वाय्वग्निविप्रादित्यापोदेवतागोषु प्रतिमिषुनं[1] वा मूत्रपुरीषामेध्यान्युदस्येत ॥

१ (ख) गोष्ठ वा पद्मम्।

यमः— प्रत्यादित्यं न मेहेत न पश्येदात्मनः शकृत् ।
दृष्ट्वा सूर्यं निरीक्षेत गामग्निं ब्राह्मणं तथा ॥
प्रत्यादित्यं प्रत्यनिलं प्रतिगाञ्च प्रतिद्विजम् ।
प्रतिसोमं प्रतिजलं प्रतिसन्ध्यञ्च नित्यशः ॥
घ्नन्ति मेहयतः प्रज्ञां प्रतिपन्थानमेव च ।
मेहयन्ति य एतासु ते भवन्ति गतायुषः ॥

हारीतः—

रथ्याचत्वरतीर्थेषु श्मशानायतनेषु च ।
अपथं समवाप्नोति आयुषा च विमुच्यते ॥

मेहयतीति शेषः ।

विष्णुः—

तिष्ठन्नातिचिरं तत्र ।

तत्र मूत्रपुरीषस्थाने ।

यमः—

नामेध्यमङ्गारैर्न भूम्याञ्चापि बर्हिषा ।

आपस्तम्बः—

आर्द्रानोषधि वनस्पतीनूर्द्ध्वमाच्छिद्य मूत्रपुरीषयोः संस्रवं[1] वर्ज्जयेत् ।

॥ इति गृहस्थरत्नाकरे मूत्रपुरीषोत्सर्गः ॥

---

१ मूले सुन्धने ।

अथ शौचं।

तत्र हारीतः—

शुष्ककाष्ठेन वा मृज्जीत। शिश्नगुदे इति शेषः।

पारस्करः—

स्वयं शीर्णेन काष्ठेन वा प्रमृज्जीत।

गोतमः—

न हरित्तृणलोष्टाभिर्मूत्रपुरीषाणामपकर्षणं कुर्य्यात्।

हारीतः—

लोष्टविधिरुक्तद्रव्यालाभे पर्णनिषेधोऽप्यसाराच्छिद्यमान-पर्ण-गोचरः।

तथा आपस्तम्बः—

अश्मना लोष्टकाष्ठार्द्रानोषधिवनस्पतीनूर्द्धानाच्छिद्य मूत्र-पुरीषयोः शुन्धनं वर्ज्जयेत्॥

देवलः—

अशौचं नोन्मृजेच्छिन्नं मलावोच्चारयोः स्वयम्।

याज्ञवल्क्य-बौधायनौ—

गृहीतशिश्नश्चोत्थाय मृद्भिरभ्युद्धृतैर्जलैः।

गन्धलेपक्षयकरं शौचं कुर्य्यादतन्द्रितः॥

अतन्द्रित आलस्यशून्यः।

ब्रह्माण्डपुराणे—

उद्धृतोदकमादाय मृत्तिकाञ्चैव वाग्यतः।

उदङ्मुखो दिवा कुर्य्याद्रात्रौ चेद्दक्षिणामुखः॥

कुर्य्याच्छौचमिति शेषः ।

तथा—

सुनिर्णिक्ते मृदं दद्यात् मृदन्ते आप एव च ।

सुनिर्णिक्ते केवलजलप्रक्षालिते लेपाद्यादौ गन्धलेपापकर्षणे शौचममेध्यस्य तदद्भिः पूर्व्वं मृदा चेति गोतमवचनात् । एवञ्च सुनिर्णिक्तपदं काष्ठादिप्रोज्झितगुदानुवादकमिति स्मृतिवचनव्याख्यानमसङ्गतमिति वैयर्थ्यात् ॥

देवलः—

धर्म्मविद्दक्षिणं हस्तमधःशौचे न योजयेत् ।

तथैव वामहस्तेन नाभेरूर्द्ध्वं न शोधयेत् ॥

प्रकृतिस्थितिरेवास्मात् कारणादुभयक्रिया ।

कारणाद्रोगादेः ।

दक्षः—

एका लिङ्गे च सव्ये त्रिरुभयोर्म्मृद्द्वयं स्मृतम् ।

सव्ये उभयोरिति च हस्ताभिप्रायेणोक्तं एतावन्मूत्रोत्सर्गाशौचम्

तिस्रोऽपाने दशैकस्मिन्नुभयोः सप्त मृत्तिकाः ।

उभयोर्हस्तयोः ।

गृहस्थाशौचमाख्यातं त्रिष्वन्येषु यथाक्रमम् ।

द्विगुणं त्रिगुणञ्चैव चतुर्थे च चतुर्गुणम् ॥

अर्द्धप्रसृतिमात्रा तु प्रथमा मृत्तिका स्मृता ।

द्वितीया च तृतीया च तदर्द्धं परिकीर्त्तितम् ॥

लिङ्गेऽप्यत्र समाख्याता त्रिपर्व्वा पूर्य्यते यया ।

दातव्यमुदकं तावद्यावत् स्यान्मृत्तिकाक्षयः ॥

सुधाद्रव्येन शुद्धिः स्यान्न क्लेशो नैव च वृथा ।

सुधाद्रव्येण सुलभद्रव्येण ।

यस्य शौचेऽपि शैथिल्यं वृत्तं तस्य परौचितम्[1] ।

मनुः—

विण्मूत्रोत्सर्गशुद्ध्यर्थं मृद्वार्यादेयमर्थवत् ।

दैहिकानां मलानाञ्च शुद्धिषु द्वादशस्वपि ॥

मनुः—

एका लिङ्गे गुदे तिस्रस्तथैकत्र करे दश ।

उभयोः सप्त दातव्या मृदः शुद्धिमभीप्सता ॥

एकत्र वामे ।

मनु-विष्णू—

वसाशुक्रमसृङ्मज्जा-मूत्रविट्कर्णविन्नखाः ।

श्लेष्माश्रु दूषिका स्वेदो द्वादशैते नृणां मलाः ॥

स्मृतिसमुच्चये मनुः—

करगृहीतपात्रेण कृत्वा मूत्रपुरीषयोः ।

तन्मूत्रसमपानीयं पीत्वा चान्द्रायणं चरेत् ॥

विष्णुपुराणे—

एका लिङ्गे गुदे तिस्रो दश वामकरे नृप ।

हस्तद्वये च सप्तान्या मृदः शौचोपपादिकाः ॥

एतच्छुद्धिर्गृहस्थानां द्विगुणं ब्रह्मचारिणाम् ।

१ (ख) शौचम् ।

त्रिगुणं वानप्रस्थानां यतीनाञ्च चतुर्गुणम् ॥
अह्निका विहितं शौचं रात्रौ तस्यार्द्धमिष्यते ।
तदर्द्धमातुरे प्रोक्तमातुरस्यार्द्धमध्वनि ॥

यम— शिश्ने त्वेका गुदे तिस्रो वामे पाणौ चतुर्दश ।
ततः पुनरुभाभ्याञ्च दातव्याः सप्त मृत्तिकाः ॥

शङ्खः—

मेहने मृत्तिकाः सप्त लिङ्गे द्वे परिकीर्त्तिते ।
एकस्मिन् विंशतिर्हस्ते द्वयोर्ज्ञेया चतुर्द्दश ॥

मेहनमत्र अपानं द्वयोर्हस्तयोः ।

तिस्रस्तु मृत्तिका देया कृत्वा तु नखशोधनम् ।
तिस्रस्तु पादयोर्देयाः शौचकामेन नित्यशः ॥
शौचमेतद्गृहस्थानां तथा गुरुनिवासिनाम् ।
द्विगुणं वानप्रस्थानां यतीनां त्रिगुणं भवेत् ॥

पैठीनसिः—

मृत्तिकां संगृह्य एका लिङ्गे अपाने पञ्च एकस्मिन् हस्ते दश उभयोः सप्त मृत्तिकाः। द्विगुणं ब्रह्मचारिणां, वनवासिनां यतीनाञ्च चतुर्गुणम्। गन्धलेपक्षयं यावत् प्रक्षाल्याचम्य प्रयतो भवति।

हारीतः—

एका लिङ्गे तिस्रोऽपाने दद्यात् मृत्तिकामादोषात् पाणी प्रक्षाल्य दश सव्ये षट् षट् पृष्ठे सप्तोभाभ्याम्। द्विगुणं ब्रह्मचारिणां त्रिगुणं वानप्रस्थानां चतुर्गुणं भिक्षूणाम्।

पृष्ठे हस्तपृष्ठे।

ब्रह्मपुराणे—

द्वे लिङ्गे मृत्तिके देये गुदे सप्त यथाक्रमम् ।
दश विंशद्वामहस्ते च तथा देयास्तु मृत्तिकाः ॥
द्वयोस्तु षोडशाऽन्यास्तु पुनः सप्त च सर्व्वदा ।
पादयोर्द्वे गृहीत्वा च सुप्रक्षालितपाणिना ॥
त्रिराचम्य ततः शुद्धः स्मृत्वा विष्णुं सनातनम् ।

बौधायनः—

मूत्रे मृदाऽद्भिः प्रक्षालनं त्रिः पाणेः, मूत्रवत् रेतसः समुत्सर्गे ।

देवलः—

यावत् साध्विति मन्येत तावच्छौचं विधीयते ।
प्रमाणं शौचसंख्यायां न शिष्टैरुपदिश्यते ॥

एतद्वचनानुसारात् मनूक्त-संख्याधिकोत्तरोत्तर-मृत्संख्यानां [1]लेपानुवृत्तिशङ्कया व्यवस्था । चतुराद्यविहितसंख्यानुष्ठाने तु संख्याधिगमनेऽपि विहितमुक्तं दक्षेण—

न्यूनाधिकं न कर्त्तव्यं शौचं शुद्धिमभीप्सता ।
प्रायश्चित्तं प्रयुज्येत विहितातिक्रमे कृतम् ॥

इति । पारिजाते तु देवलवचनानां [2]चतुराश्रमेषु स्त्रीशूद्रानुपनीतविषयत्वाद्व्याख्यातम् । तच्च संख्यादेरश्रुतेः । उदकविषयं वा—

---

१ (क) गन्धलेपक्षयकरसंख्यया ।
२ (ख) चतुराश्रमेतरविषयं स्त्रीशूद्रानुपीतविषयं वा ।

हातव्यमुदकं तावत् यावत् स्यान्मृत्तिकाक्षयः ।

इति दक्षेणाप्युक्तेः । इत्युक्तम् ।

अनुक्तपक्षेऽपि वामकरपृष्ठेऽपि षट् मृत्तिका देयाः । षट् पृष्ठत इति हारीतवचनात् ।

शौचानन्तरं शङ्खलिखितौ—

कमण्डलुमुपस्पृश्य प्रक्षाल्य पाणि-पादौ वाचमु[1]त्सृज्य मनसा ईशानं ध्यायेत् । ईशान ईश्वरः ।

शौचानन्तरं हारीतः—

तिसृभिः पादौ प्रक्षाल्य गोमयेन वा कमण्डलुं परिमृज्य पूर्ववदुपस्पृश्यादित्यं सोममग्निं वीक्षेत ।

अत्र दिवा आदित्यं रात्रौ सोमं तयोरभावे अग्निमिति ज्ञेयम् ।

आपस्तम्बः—

अह्नि शौचं यथा प्रोक्तं निश्यर्द्धन्तु तदिष्यते ।
पथि पादस्तु विज्ञेय आर्त्तः कुर्य्याद्यथाबलम् ॥

न पश्येदात्मनः शकृदित्यनुवृत्तौ गौतमः—

दृष्ट्वा सूर्य्यं निरीक्षेत गामग्निं ब्राह्मणं तथा ।

यच्चैव व्यासः—

शौचं कृत्वा मूत्रोच्चारं न पश्येत ।

दक्षः—

यथा शौचं दिवा शौचमर्द्धं रात्रौ विधीयते

१ (ख) वाचम् ।

आतुरस्य तदर्द्धं स्यात् तदर्द्धन्तु पथि स्मृतम् ॥

छन्दोगपरिशिष्टः—

यस्मिन् स्थाने कृतं शौचं वारिणा च विशोधयेत् ।
न शुद्धिस्तु भवेत्तस्य मृत्तिकां यो न शोधयेत् ॥

विष्णुपुराणे—

वल्मीकमूषिकोत्खातां मृदमन्तर्जलात्तथा ।
शौचावशिष्टां गेहाच्च नादद्याल्लेपसम्भवाम् ॥
अन्तःप्राण्यवपन्नाञ्च हलोत्खाताञ्च पार्थिव ।
परित्यजेन्मृदस्त्वेताः सकलाः शौचसाधने ॥

अन्तःप्राण्यवपन्नां अन्तर्मध्ये प्राणिभिः कीटादिभिर्युक्ताम् ।

यमः—

आहरेन्मृत्तिकां विप्रः कूलात् ससिकतां तथा ।
नाखूत्कृष्टां न वल्मीकां न पांशुलां न कर्द्दमाम् ॥
न मार्गान्नोषराच्चैव शौचशिष्टां परस्य तु ।
एतास्तु वर्ज्जयेद्विद्वान् वृथा शौचं हि तत् स्मृतम् ॥

आखूत्कृष्टां मूषिकोत्कृष्टाम् ।

इति गृहस्थरत्नाकरे शौचतरङ्गः ॥

Appendix B

Hindi translation of Mutrapurishotsarga

मूत्र–मलत्याग

इस प्रसंग विष्णुपुराण में –

हे राजन् ! तब तड़के सुबह उठकर मैत्रक्रिया (मलत्याग) करना चाहिए जो नैर्ऋत्य (दक्षिण–पश्चिम) दिशा में उतने दूर मे करना उचित है जितने दूर बाण फेकने से पृथ्वी पर गिरे। वहाँ देर तक न ठहरें एवं कुछ न बोलें।

'कल्य' का अर्थ उषाकाल है, 'मैत्र' हुआ विष्ठा का त्याग क्योंकि मलत्याग के देवता मित्र (सूर्य) हैं, जिनके सम्बन्ध से वह क्रिया मैत्र कहलाती है।

———

याज्ञवल्क्य –

जूठा, विष्ठा, मूत्र और पैर धोने के पानी को दूर में फेकें।

———

आपस्तम्ब –

1. मूत्र और मल का त्याग दक्षिण दिशा में या दक्षिण के समीप में करें' इस वाक्य में जाकर' यह जोड़ें। दक्षिण के समीप अर्थात् नैर्ऋत्य (दक्षिण–पश्चिम) दिशा में।

2. सूर्यास्त हो जाने पर गाँव से बाहर, घर से दूर में मूत्र एवं मल त्याग करें। 'आवसथ' का अर्थ घर एवम् 'आरात्' का दूर होता है।

———

मनु –

घर से दूर ही मूत्रत्याग करें, बाहर ही पैर धोवें और जूठे अन्न और कचरे को दूर ही फेकें।

'पादावसेचन' का अर्थ है पैर धोना। 'निषेक' का अर्थ है जूठे वस्तुओं को फेकना।

लकड़ी, पत्ते, ढेले या खढ़ से जमीन को ढ़ँक कर मलत्याग करें और उस समय नियमपूर्वक वाणी को नियन्त्रित कर

(चुप रहकर) शरीर को सकुचा कर कपड़े से सिर से मुँह तक ढ़ँके रहें अर्थात् मुरेठा बान्धें जिससे कान, नाक एवं मुँह ढ़ँक जाय।

'लकड़ी आदि से दूर तक ढ़ँक कर' यह उपर्युक्त श्लोक के पूर्वभाग का तात्पर्य हुआ। 'उच्चरेत्' का अर्थ हुआ मल का त्याग करें। 'प्रयतः' अर्थात् पवित्रतापूर्वक वाणी को रोक कर, यह अर्थ हुआ। 'संवीत' हुआ कण्ठलम्बित यज्ञोपवीत रखना, क्योंकि "संवीत मनुष्य सम्बन्धित कृत्य काल में होता है" ऐसा तैत्तिरीय शाखीय वेद में कहा गया है। यह तो द्विवस्त्र पक्ष में (दो वस्त्र रखने पर) करना है। एक वस्त्र रहने पर तो यज्ञोपवीत को कान पर लटकाना उचित है।

———

सांख्यायन गृहसूत्र में लिखा है –

यदि एक वस्त्र ही पहने हों तो यज्ञोपवीत को कान पर रख कर मल–मूत्र त्याग करें।

जैसा कि यम ने कहा है –

यज्ञोपवीत (जनेऊ) को कण्ठ से लगाकर पीठ पर लटकाकर गृहस्थ मूत्र–मल का त्याग करें अथवा जनेऊ को कान पर ठीक से रखकर करें।

———

बौधायन –

सूखे खढ़ अथवा यज्ञ के अनुपयुक्त काठ से भूमि को ढ़ँक कर दिन में उत्तर की ओर और रात में दक्षिण की ओर मुँह कर सिर को बान्धकर पैखाना करें या पेशाव करें।

'अयाज्ञिक' का अर्थ हुआ यज्ञ में उपयुक्त होने वाले कुश, पलाश इत्यादि से अतिरिक्त। 'अवमेहेत' का अर्थ हुआ मूत्र त्याग करें।

———

विष्ठा एवं मूत्र के त्याग के सन्दर्भ में वायुपुराण में कहा गया है –

सूखे तिनके, काठ, पत्ते या बाँस के पत्ते या मिट्टी के पात्रों से भूमि को ढ़ँक कर ही मूत्र–मल त्याग करें।

———

हारीत –

नाक और मुँह को ढ़ँक कर मिट्टी की झोली को गरदन से लटका कर दाहिने बाँह के पास भूमि पर कमण्डलु (लोटा) रखकर मलत्याग करें।

'मृत्पात्री' का अर्थ है मिट्टी रखने की छोटी झोली। 'उत्सृजेत्' के साथ मलमूत्र का अन्वय है।

———

मनु –

मूत्र और मल का त्याग दिन में उत्तराभिमुख, रात को दक्षिणाभिमुख एवं दोनों सन्ध्याओं (सुबह और शाम) में दिन के समान करना चाहिए।

———

संख्यायनगृह्यसूत्र –

सूर्य के सम्मुख न रहते हुए जिससे जघन (पेडू) उनके सामने न आबे, इस तरह मूत्र मल त्याग करें।

'न जघनेन' इससे स्पष्ट होता है कि सूर्य के सम्मुख 'जघन' जहाँ न पड़े वहाँ करना चाहिए।

———

यम –

पूर्वाह्ण में उत्तर की ओर, अपराह्ण में पूरब की ओर, मध्याह्न में उत्तर की ओर और रात में दक्षिण की ओर मुँह कर मलत्याग करना चाहिए।

———

देवल –

सुबह में हमेशा उत्तर की ओर, सायं (दिन के अंतिम भाग) में दक्षिण की ओर होकर विष्ठा और मूत्र का त्याग करें और सन्ध्याओं में करना ही नहीं चाहिये।

उनमें यह व्यवस्था है – देवल के वाक्य के बल से प्रातः एवं सायंकाल तीन–तीन मुहूर्त्त (2 घंटा 44 मिनट = तीन मुहूर्त्त) में उत्तर मुँह होकर एवं यमवचन तो उससे अतरिक्त पूर्वाह्ण में पश्चिम मुँह को बतलाने वाला है।

———

मनु –

छाया में तथा अन्धकार में रात या दिन हो तो द्विज को चाहिए कि अपनी सुविधा के अनुसार किसी भी दिशा की ओर मुँह करके मलत्याग करें और जान का खतरा या भय होने पर भी ऐसा ही करें।

छाया एवं अन्धकार में प्राणसंकट और बाघ आदि के भय रहने पर दिशा की ओर के नियम का आदर नहीं करें।

फिर वहीं लिखा है – रास्ते पर, भस्म पर, चारागाह पर, फार से जोते हुए खेत में, जल में, नदी में (या चिता भूमि में) और पहाड़ पर मल–मूत्र त्याग न करें।

यहाँ मूत्र शब्द अजहत्स्वार्था लक्षणा (जिसमें अपने अर्थ को न छोड़ते हुए अन्य अर्थ भी लिया जाता है) के द्वारा मल का भी उपलक्षण (परिचायक,बोधक) है। 'चित्याम्' का अर्थ अग्निचयन स्थान या चिता है।

उसी तरह – जर्जर मन्दिर में, दीमक के ढेर पर, जीव से युक्त गड्ढे में, चलते हुए, खड़ा होकर, नदी तट पर, पर्वत की चोटी पर, वायु अग्नि विप्र सूर्य और जल को देखते हुए कभी भी विष्ठा और मूत्र का त्याग न करें।

'न पर्वते' इस पूर्वोक्त वचन से पर्वत का निषेध होने पर भी उसके मस्तक का निषेध बहुतायत के अभिप्राय से है। जहाँ पर्वत पर न करना असम्भव हो वहाँ चोटी को छोड़ने का अभिप्राय है ऐसा पारिजात नामक ग्रन्थ में हैं। वायु आदि को देखते हुए से सम्मुख उपलब्ध समझना चाहिए।

हारीत –

चबूतरा एवं द्वार के समीप मूत्र–मल त्याग नहीं करना चाहिए। यह न तो तीर्थ में, न फसल लगे खेत में, न यज्ञ भूमि में और न ही यज्ञ के उपयोग में आने वाले वृक्ष के नीचे ही करे।

चत्वर का अर्थ हुआ अनेक लोगों के बैठने का स्थान, किसी के मत से कौए आदि के लिए अन्न देने का स्थान। उपद्वार का अर्थ हुआ द्वारसमीप। तीर्थे अर्थात् पवित्र (धार्मिक) स्थान में, दूसरों के मत से जल गिरने के मार्ग में।

देवल –

वापी (वाउली), कूप, नदी, पशु बाँधने का स्थान, चिता के वृक्ष, आवास, जल, अग्नि, धातु (काँसा आदि) और श्मशान में मल एवं मूत्र का त्याग न करें।

वापी आदि पद बिना जलवालों का बोधक है क्योंकि जल का अलग से उल्लेख है। चैत्य हुआ गाँव भर के व्यवहार में आने वाला वृक्ष। आवास हुआ वास का परिसर।

यम –

पोखरा, तालाब, नदी, झरना, पर्वत, गोवर, भस्म और हल से जोते खेत को छोड़कर मल–मूत्र त्याग करें।

पल्वल का अर्थ छोटा तालाब होता है। तडाग कृत्रिम (बनाया हुआ, प्राकृतिक नहीं) सरोवर को कहते हैं।

भूसा, अंगार, खप्पर, देवालय, राजमार्ग, श्मशान, खेत, खलिहान, छाया और चौराहे पर वेग रहने पर भी मूत्र एवं मल का त्याग न करें।

उपरुद्ध = विष्ठा और मूत्र से पीड़ित रहने पर मूत्र–मल त्याग हेतु उपयोग न करें। रास्ते पर न करें इस कथन के रहने पर भी राजमार्ग और चौराहे का उल्लेख अत्यन्त दोष दिखाने हेतु हुआ है। 'श्वभ्र' का अर्थ हैं फटे हुए भू–भाग।

वसिष्ठ –

बोये हुए खेत में और चिकने घास वाली छाया में मल–मूत्र त्यागना निषिद्ध है।

शाद्वल हुआ हरे चिकने भू–भाग।

ऊसर में, गन्दा जगह में, फुलवाड़ी में, पानी में, टीला पर और आकाश में (पेड़ या कोठा पर से या बिना घेरे में) मल–मूत्र का त्याग न करें।

आकाश से तात्पर्य है अटारी पर से नीचे गिराना। इसी तरह – वायु, चन्द्र, सूर्य, स्त्री, गुरु, ब्राह्मण की विपरीत दिशा में ...।

आपस्तब –

छाया में मूत्र और मल का कार्य त्याग दें, किन्तु अपनी छाया में कर सकते हैं।

अपनी छाया के प्रति यह जोड़ देना चाहिए। इससे अपनी छाया में यह दोष नहीं है।

उसी तरह वहीं (आपस्तम्ब के ग्रन्थ में ही) – जूते पहन कर मूत्र–मल न त्यागें।

फिर वहीं – गाय और देवता के सम्मुख मूत्र–मल का कर्म छोड़ दें।

———

गौतम –

वायु, अग्नि, ब्राह्मण, सूर्य, जल, देवता, और गाय के सम्मुख या इन्हें देखते हुए मूत्र–मल या अशुचि (कफ आदि) न फेकें।

———

यम –

आदित्य (सूर्य) के सम्मुख मल–मूत्र त्याग न करें और अपनी विष्ठा का निरीक्षण न करें। यदि देखलें तो पवित्र होकर सूर्य, अग्नि, गाय या ब्राह्मण का दर्शन करें।

चन्द्र, जल, संध्या और रास्ता के सम्मुख या पास में मल–मूत्र त्यागने वाले की बुद्धि नष्ट होती है। अज्ञानता से जो ऐसा करते हैं उनका आयु समाप्त हो जाता है।

———

हारीत –

गली, चबूतरा, तीर्थ, श्मशान और मन्दिर परिसर में मल–मूत्र त्यागने से विपरीत दिशा में जाते हैं और आयु से हीन हो जाते है।

———

विष्णु –

वहाँ देर तक न रूकें।

वहाँ अर्थात् मूत्र–मल के स्थान में।

———

यम –

अपवित्र वस्तु को अंगारों या कुशों से साफ न करे।

———

आपस्तम्ब –

भींगे लता, फसल आदि और वनस्पति को ऊपर से काटकर मूत्र–मल का त्याग न करे।

।।गृहस्थरत्नाकर में मूत्र–मल के त्याग का प्रकरण समाप्त हुआ।।

शौच प्रकरण

इसमें हारीत का वचन है –

सूखी लकड़ी से पोछें।

'लिंग और गुदा को' यह वाक्य का शेष है।

पारस्कर ने लिखा है –

स्वतः जीर्ण हुए काठ से पोछें।

गौतम –

हरे खढ़ और ढेले से मूत्र और मल को साफ न करें।

हारीत –

यदि विहित वस्तु न मिले तो ढेले से भी पोछ सकते हैं। पत्ते का निषेध भी असार (कोमल) एवम् तोड़े हुए पत्ते के विषय में है।

वैसा आपस्तम्ब ने भी कहा है –

पत्थर से या ढेला, काठ, बिना सूखे घास एवं वनस्पति को ऊपर से तोड़ कर मूत्र–मल को साफ न करें।

देवल –

पेशाव और मलत्याग में अशुद्ध लिंग को मत रगड़े।

याज्ञवलक्य और बौधायन –

लिंग को पकड़ के मलत्याग स्थान से उठकर मिट्टी और जलाशय से लाये हुए जल से सावधानी से शौच करें जिससे गन्ध, नष्ट हो जाय।

'अतन्द्रित' का अर्थ हुआ आलस्य न करते हुए। 'उद्‌धृत' से तात्पर्य है कि तालाब में शौच न करें।

ब्रह्माण्ड पुराण में –

जलाशय से निकाले हुए पानी लेकर तथा मिट्टी लेकर चुप रहते हुए दिन में उत्तर की ओर और रात में दक्षिण ओर होकर शौच करें। 'कुर्यात्' का शेष शौच है।

तथा – जल से पूरा–पूरी साफ होने पर मिट्टी लगाबें और उसके बाद जल से साफ करें।

'सुनिर्णिक्त' का अर्थ हुआ केवल जल से धोने पर, लेप आदि में – गन्ध लेप को हटाने में अशुद्धि का शौच तो पहले जल से और तब मिट्टी और जल से साफ करें, यह गौतम के वचन का आशय है।

इस तरह 'सुनिर्णिक्त' पद काठ आदि से पोछे हुए गुदा को साफ करने को व्यक्त करता है, यह स्मृतिवचन का व्याख्यान असंगत है, क्योंकि वह व्यर्थ हो रहा है।

देवल मुनि का कथन है –

धर्मज्ञानी को चाहिए कि दाहिने हाथ को नीचे की शौचक्रिया में न लगावें, उसी तरह वायें हाथ से नाभि से ऊपर को साफ न करें। प्रकृतिस्थ (स्वस्थ) रहने पर यह नियम है, परन्तु किसी कारण वश दोनो हाथों से ऊपर या नीचे की शुद्धि की जा सकती है। यहाँ 'कारण' पद से रोग, आकिस्मक आफत आदि लेना चाहिए।

दक्ष मुनि का कथन है –

मूत्र त्याग के बाद जल से शौच करने के अनन्तर मिट्टी एवं जल से एक बार लिंग को शुद्ध करें, वाँयाँ हाथ को तीन बार एवं दोनों हाथों को दो बार मिट्टी एवं जल से शुद्ध करें।

यहाँ 'सव्ये' एवं 'उभयोः' का कथन हाथ के विषय में कहा गया है। इतना मूत्र त्याग का शौच हुआ।

मल त्याग करने पर एक वार लिंग में, तीन वार गुद में, दश वार वायें हाथ में एवं सात वार दोनों हाथों में मिट्टी एवं जल से शुद्ध करें। यहाँ 'उभयोः' से तात्पर्य दोनों हाथों से है।

यह जो कहा गया है वह गृहस्थ के लिये है। इस से भिन्न तीनों आश्रमियों के लिये क्रमशः इससे दूना, तिगुना और

चारगुना शौच का विधान है। अर्थात् ब्रह्मचारी, वानप्रस्थी और संन्यासी के लिये क्रमशः अधिक शुद्धि आवश्यक है।

पहली वार आधा प्रसृति (लप = एक हाथ को फैलाकर अंगुलियों को सटाने पर वस्तु के माप को 'प्रसृति' कहते हैं) मिट्टी लें, दूसरी उससे आधी, तीसरी उससे आधी कही गयी है।

लिंग शुद्धि में चारों अंगुलियों पर आने वाली मिट्टी लेने का विधान है। तब तक जल देते रहें जब तक मिट्टी पूरा–पूरी धुल जाय। वारीक मिट्टी से शुद्धि करें जिससे कष्ट न हो।

'सुधाद्रव्य' का अर्थ हुआ सुलभ द्रव्य। अर्थात् चिकनी मिट्टी को सुखाकर पीस कर सूखे पतले कपड़े से छान कर छोटी झोली में रख लें और उसी का उपयोग करें।

जिसे शौच करने में भी शिथिलता है, उसका आचरण ही परीक्षित हो जाता है कि वह किसी कार्य का अधिकारी नही हो सकता।

———

मनु –

मल–मूत्र त्याग के इन्द्रिय की तथा शरीर के घाम, चर्वी आदि बारह प्रकार के मलों की शुद्धि में आवश्यकतानुसार मिट्टी लेनी चाहिए।

———

मनु –

शुद्धि चाहनेवालों को चाहिए कि लिंग में एक, गुदा में तीन, वायें हाथ में दश और दोनों हाथों में सात वार मिट्टी देवें। 'एकत्र' से तात्पर्य है वायाँ हाथ से ।

———

मनु और विष्णु –

वसा (माँस की चर्वी), वीर्य, शोणित, मज्जा (हड्डी की चर्वी), मूत्र, मल, कान के मल (गुज्जी), नेटा (नकटी, शुष्क कफ), कफ (थूक, खखार, पीक आदि), आँसू, आँख का मल (काँची) और घाम– ये बारह मल मनुष्य के होते हैं।

———

स्मृतिसमुच्चय में विष्णु का वचन है –

हाथ में रखे हुए पात्र से मूत्र–मल की शुद्धि करने पर

उसमें बचा हुआ पानी मूत्र के समान अशुद्ध हो जाता है। उसे पीने पर चान्द्रायणव्रत से शुद्धि होती है।

———

विष्णुपुराण में –

एक लिंग में, तीन गुदा में, दस वायाँ हाथ में, सात दोनों हाथों में शौच हेतु मिट्टी लगानी चाहिए। यह शुद्धि गृहस्थों की है, ब्रह्मचारियों को इससे दूनी, वानप्रस्थियों को तिगुनी और संन्यासियों को चौगुनी मिट्टी लगानी चाहिए। दिन में जितने शौच का विधान है, रात में उससे आधा करना चाहिए। उससे आधा आतुरों (दुर्बलों,व्याधिग्रस्तों) को और उससे आधा राह में करना चाहिए।

———

यम –

लिंग में एक, गुदा में तीन, वायाँ हाथ में चौदह और दोनों हाथों में सात वार मिट्टी देवें।

———

शंख मुनि –

गुदा में सात, लिंग में दो, वायाँ हाथ में बीस और दोनों हाथों में चौदह मिट्टी दें।

यहाँ 'मेहन' का अर्थ गुदा है और 'द्वयोः' से दोनों हाथ समझें।

प्रतिदिन नह को शुद्ध कर तीन वार हाथ में मिट्टी लगावें और धोंवे। पैर में भी तीन बार मिट्टी जल लगा कर शुद्ध होवें।

यह शौच गृहस्थ एवं गुरु के आश्रम में रहने वाले शिष्य के लिये है। वानप्रस्थी इससे दूना और संन्यासी चौगुना शुद्ध करें।

———

पैठीनसि का वचन है –

मिट्टी को चुनकर एक लिंग में, पाँच गुदा में, वायें हाथ में दस और दोनों हाथों में सात वार लगावें। ब्रह्मचारियों को इससे दूना, वनवासियों और संन्यासियों को चार गुना शौच करना चाहिए। गन्धलेप का क्षय होने तक धोकर आचमन करने के बाद शुद्ध होता है।

———

हारीत –

एक मिट्टी लिंग में, तीन गुदा में लगाकर धोते रहें जब तक गन्ध दोष मिट न जाय। दोनों हाथों को धोकर वायें में दस, हाथ के पीछे छः–छः तथा सात मिट्टी दोनों हाथों में दें। ब्रह्मचारियों को इससे दूनी, वानप्रस्थियों को तिगुनी और संन्यासियों को चार गुनी मिट्टी लगानी चाहिए। 'पृष्ठे' से तात्पर्य है हाथ के पिछले भाग से ।

ब्रह्मपुराण में –

लिंग में दो मिट्टी देनी चाहिए, गुदा में क्रमशः सात, वायें हाथ में बाइस, दोनों हाथों में सोलह, फिर सात मिट्टी लगावें और दोनों पैरों में दो मिट्टी लगाकर जल से धोकर हाथ को फिर से धोते हुए तीन वार आचमन कर सनातन विष्णु का स्मरण कर शुद्धि होती है।

बौधायन –

मूत्र त्याग में मिट्टी और जल से धोवें, तीन बार हाथों का प्रक्षालन करें। वीर्य त्याग में मूत्र त्याग के समान शुद्धि करें।

देवल –

जब तक मन मान जाय कि शुद्ध हो गया तब तक शौच करना चाहिए। शौच की संख्या का निर्धारण मान्यों के द्वारा नहीं की जाती है।

इस वचन के अनुसार मनु के द्वारा कही गयी संख्या से अधिक आगे–आगे के स्मृतिकारों के द्वारा मिट्टी की अधिकता के कथन का तात्पर्य है कि गन्धलेप की अनुवृत्ति न रह जाय, इस लिये यह व्यवस्था दी गयी है। चार–पाँच आदि संख्या स्वीकार करने पर तो संख्या का अनुपालन करना ही चाहिए, जैसा कि दक्ष ने कहा है –

शुद्धि चाहने वालों को शौच के विषय में विहित संख्या से कम–वेशी नहीं करना चाहिए। विहित संख्या के अनुपालन न करने पर प्रायश्चित्त करना होता है।

'पारिजात' ग्रन्थ में तो देवल के वचनों की व्याख्या इस

प्रकार की गयी है कि यह चारों आश्रमों में स्त्री, शुद्र तथा अनुपनीत (बिना उपनयन के वटुक) के विषय में है क्योंकि वहाँ संख्या का निर्धारण नहीं है। अथवा जल के विषय में वह वचन है क्योंकि – तब तक जल देना चाहिए, जब तक मिट्टी पूर्णतः साफ न हो जाय – ऐसा दक्ष ने कहा है, यह भी वहाँ ('पारिजात' में) कहा गया है।

मनु के द्वारा कथित पक्ष में भी वायें हाथ के पीछे भी छः मिट्टियाँ देनी चाहिए, हारीत के वचन से भी यही आता है कि छः हस्तपृष्ठ में भी मिट्टियाँ आवश्यक हैं।

शौच के बाद शंख लिखित ने कहा है – कमण्डलु (लोटा) को पकड़ के हाथ–पाँव धोकर वाणी को व्यक्त कर मन से ईशान (महादेव) का ध्यान करें। यहाँ 'ईशान' ईश्वर हैं।

शौच के बाद हारीत ने लिखा है –

तीन मिट्टी से दोनों पैरों को धोकर, मिट्टी या गोबर से कमण्डलु को माँज कर पूर्व की भाँति आचमन कर सूर्य, चन्द्र और अग्नि का दर्शन करें।

यहाँ दिन में सूर्य, रात में चाँद और इन दोनों के अभाव में अग्नि को देखें, ऐसा जानें।

आपस्तम्ब –

दिन में जिस तरह का शौच कहा गया है, रात में उसका आधा करना चाहिए, राह में उसका चौथाई और आर्त्त (अस्वस्थ, अशक्त) रहने पर जितना हो सके उतना ही करें।

अपनी विष्ठा का निरीक्षण नहीं करना चाहिए, जिस सन्दर्भ में गौतम ने कहा है–

मल को देखने पर सूर्य, गाय, अग्नि तथा ब्राह्मण को देखें।

इसी विषय में गौतम कहते हैं –

शौच करके मूत्र एवं मल को न देखें।

———

दक्ष –

जैसा शौच दिन में कहा गया है, उसका आधा रात में करें, आतुर (पीड़ित) व्यक्ति उसका आधा करें और रास्ते में उसका आधा करें।

———

ऋषिश्रृंग –

जिस स्थान में शौच किया हो उसे जल से धो दें। उस व्यक्ति की शुद्धि तब तक नहीं होती जब तक कि उस भूमि को शुद्ध न करते हैं।

———

विष्णुपुराण में –

दीमक, चूहा आदि के द्वारा निकाली गयी मिट्टी, पानी के तले की मिट्टी, शौच से बची हुई मिट्टी, घर की मिट्टी, जिस मिट्टी में जीव समायें हों और हल से जोती हुई मिट्टी को हे राजन्! शौच के लिए उपयोग न करें।

'अन्तःप्रण्यवपन्नाम्' का अर्थ हुआ भीतर में कीड़ा आदि से युक्त।

———

यम –

ब्राह्मण को चाहिए कि जल के तट से बालू युक्त मिट्टी का ग्रहण करें। न तो चूहे की, न दीमक की, न धूल भरी, न कीचड़, न रास्ते की, न ऊसर भूमि की और न ही दूसरे के शौच से बची हुई मिट्टी का उपयोग करें। विचारवान् व्यक्ति इन मिट्टी का त्याग करें क्योंकि इन से शौच करना व्यर्थ है।

'आखूत्कृष्टाम्' का अर्थ हुआ चूहा के द्वारा निकाली हुई मिट्टी ।

।। इति गृहस्थरत्नाकर में शौचतरंग समाप्त।।